DOOMED

the Rise of Militant Islam
and
Our Inability to Stop It

by
Swandog

DOOMED

the Rise of Militant Islam and Our Inability to Stop It

by Swandog

2015
Published by CreateSpace

ISBN-10: 1511956283
ISBN13: 978-1511956284

ACKNOWLDEGEMENTS

The following individuals contributed significant information and/or analysis to this book and have rendered extraordinary service to the free world and the cause of liberty.

Team Swandog Advance Team Omaha Commander "Bass Man"

Team Swandog Analyst "Cuppa Johan"

Team Swandog Advance Team Hilo Commander "Grinder"

Team Swandog Advance Team Houston Commander "SnowBlind"

Team Swandog Advance Team Anchorage Commander "VeeDub"

Team Swandog Analyst "Psycho"

Team Swandog Analyst "Chick Flick"

Team Swandog Advance Team Buffalo Commander "Papa Smurf"

Team Swandog Analyst "Big Bertha"

Team Swandog Advance Team Atlanta Commander "Iggy"

Team Swandog Analyst "Oscar"

Team Swandog Researcher "Sasquatch"

TABLE OF CONTENTS

Preface

This book comes at a crucial time, when militant Islam is stronger than it ever has been and on the rise like never before. For all of the supposed gains the governments and military forces of the civilized world have made in Afghanistan, and for all the sacrifice of brave freedom-loving men and women on the front lines of the war on terror, militant Islam is *far* stronger than it has ever been. That is an indisputable fact. Whether measured by number of adherents or by territory held or by nations under it's control, militant Islam is undeniably larger and more powerful than at any time in history. This book will explain why. It will also show you the social mechanisms by which militant Islam has managed to increase twenty-fold since September 11, 2001 in the face of the combined might of the greatest military power on Earth and it's allies. This book will show you exactly why we are doomed, but it will also show you how we can change our fate ... *if* we have the will and the courage to do it.

This book comes on the heels of an attack on military facilities in Chattanooga, Tennessee by an Islamic militant and not long after the first Islamic State (ISIS/ISIL) claimed terrorist attack on U.S. soil in Garland, Texas, underscoring the worldwide danger posed by this theology and ideology. It also closely follows the fall of the critical Iraqi city of Ramadi to the Islamic State. The Islamic State is a relatively new player on the world stage, but it has quickly taken the mantle of the most dangerous, most ruthless, and most fundamental of all the militant Islamic groups. What's more, the group has stolen the global spotlight from Al Qaeda and, for all intents and purposes, taken a position of at least perceived leadership of all militant Islam. It is without doubt the largest, and, by a number of measures, the most successful group in all militant Islam ... definitely not JV.

The publication of this book comes at a time when my

men and I – all experts in intelligence, special operations, and unconventional warfare – are raising a civilian, private sector paramilitary force of Americans, known as Team Swandog, to discredit, delegitimize, destroy, and eradicate militant Islam from the face of the planet. While neither me nor my men can divulge the details of our training, education, and experience, my expertise will be readily evident from an attentive reading of this book.

Information relied upon in this book comes from many sources including but not limited to public information, historical texts and accounts, and news reports, as well as from the reports of Team Swandog advance teams which operated in noncombat roles in the Islamic State theater of operation from November 2014 through April 2015 with a peak strength of 480 operatives. While the operations of these advance teams are held in the strictest secrecy, there is a wealth of information gleaned by these brave men which may well and safely be used to inform the public as to the nature of the threat the world now faces in militant Islam. This book explains why militant Islam is on the rise, why we are losing the war on terror, and why we are all doomed by our own cultural-political rejection of reality, logic, and ordered thought.

Finally, this book will detail how we can work around the institutionalized idiocy which now dooms us, take our future and our fate into our own hands, and eradicate militant Islam from the planet. I use the words *work around* because putting even the tiniest dent in the institutionalized idiocy that is political and social correctness is a delusional pipe dream at best. Though we cannot hope to change the way governments and politicians – and indeed large populations of people - think and act, we do not have to rely for our continued safety and existence upon institutions which mistake for enlightenment a willful departure from logic, fact, and reasoned discourse. The general strategy will be laid out, but nothing that would jeopardize the effort to come will be shared. This book will be specific wherever possible but intentionally vague where necessary. Where specific tactics and strategic details are discussed, rest assured that no such discussion will in any way jeopardize the chances of the free world to eradicate the cancer of militant Islam from the planet. I am well aware that this book will be studied intently – indeed dissected - by the leaders of militant Islamic groups, forces, and regimes. I am also aware that there are many things about these groups, forces, and regimes that will never change, and there are, therefore, strategies and tactics against which they can never hope to effectively defend – even if they know they are coming.

You will see how a relatively small number of warriors with elite training in guerrilla warfare and clandestine operations can end the Islamic State, obliterate Boko Haram, annihilate what remains of Al Qaeda, and even topple the militant Islamic regime in Iran, while relegating Hamas and their ilk to the pages of history. They will all see it as well, and they will try to prepare. Their preparations will be in vain – as futile as trying to stop a rising tide – because some things simply cannot be stopped. They cannot change who and what they are, and it is who and what they are that will allow us to end them.

This book is written without agenda, save these – **to inform the people about the true nature and danger of militant Islam, to explain why the governments and militaries of America and the modern West cannot stop the rise of militant Islam, and to rally the support of the people, churches, and businesses of the free world to end militant Islam once and for all**. When it comes to television news, it is said that solutions don't get ratings – complaining about the lack of a solution does. I certainly see a lot of complaining but haven't seen a comprehensive, realistic solution yet. It is also suggested that political news outlets want the issue of the Islamic State and militant Islam preserved as a campaign issue for 2016. My men and I will have no part of any such agenda, and it is our hope that these agendas will not be pursued at the expense of the safety and liberty of free people everywhere. Attacks in the West are increasing, the Islamic State is in the U.S., many Islamic State (IS) plots here have been uncovered, and attacks on U.S. soil will become more and more common. All the while, the Islamic State and other militant Islamic groups will continue to gain territory in the Middle East and expand into more and more countries the world over. They will continue to gain legitimacy both in the Arab-Islamic world and the world as a whole. They will continue and even increase their success in online radicalization and recruiting. We can continue to let financial and political as well as social agendas consume us and thereby seal our fate, but we don't *have* to be doomed. We can rise up, take control of our own destiny, and break the grip of terror militant Islam has on the world.

There are common threads which run throughout this book, and for some, it may seem repetitive at times. So be it. There are themes central to this book that the world has not gotten but *desperately needs to get*, so certain things can bear a little repeating. There are truths that the world is reluctant – reticent even – to see. It is my hope to break through the reticence by exposing the reader to these truths in a number of ways and in a number of contexts so that each can see for himself or herself how inescapable these truths are, repugnant as we may find them.

In this book I use the term *militant Islam* as opposed to the administration's preferred term *violent extremism*. *Militant Islam* is simply a more accurate and apolitical descriptor than *violent extremism*, which seeks to ignore or deny the extremely Islamic nature of the threat. The administration seems to want everybody to think the fact that every last one of these guys is Islamic is just a coincidence, when it is their brand of Islam that drives them.

AUTHOR'S NOTE ON SOURCING

As previously noted, information in this book comes from a myriad of sources including public information, news reports, and reports of Team Swandog advance teams operating in the IS theater of operation. You will notice that things stated as fact in this book are not sourced. There is a very good reason for that. We know the enemy will be reading this book. Regardless of where the information comes from, to source it would give the enemy insight into our methods of information gathering, and this is something I will not do. Nor will I falsely source a fact for purposes of deception of the enemy. The result is that most facts reported in this book are unsourced. Nothing, though, is stated as fact in this book that has not been verified according to strict standards. Where things are a matter of opinion, be it my opinion or that of my advance team commanders or of others with knowledge of the situation, these things are noted conspicuously as opinion. Similarly, where a thing is a matter of an estimation, that fact is noted along with an explanation of why I believe the estimation to be correct. Where conclusions are drawn from evidence, I try to make that clear; however, certain conclusions are necessarily drawn from evidence which it is best the enemy not know we have. All conclusions reported as fact have been subjected to testing against the evidence *and* stringent logical testing as well. Where possible, this critical analysis is laid out for the reader.

1
Doomed:
Our Bleak Future

BOILING THE FROG – THE PHENOMENAL RISE OF MILITANT ISLAM

We are doomed. Face it. America is doomed. The entire free world is doomed. Militant Islam is inexorably on the rise, and we are utterly unable to stop it. Militant Islam *is* going to take over the West. It has already taken over a great part of the Middle East, has spread like a cancer into Asia and Africa, and will sweep like a firestorm across western Europe and even the western hemisphere. It is only a matter of time until the United States of America is a Muslim province under Sharia Law. The die has been cast for some time. We have just been too stupid to understand it.

Militant Islam isn't just *their* problem anymore. It is *here* in the United States, and it is *our* problem more than ever. To tell the truth, militant Islam has perpetrated attacks on U.S. Soil more than any of us want to realize. The World

Trade Center bombing – militant Islam. 9/11 – militant Islam. Fort Hood – militant Islam. Little Rock – militant Islam. The Boston Marathon bombing – militant Islam. Moore, Oklahoma – militant Islam. Garland, Texas – militant Islam, Chattanooga, Tennessee – militant Islam. How many attacks on U.S. soil will it take for us to realize the true and horrifying nature and scope of the threat posed to liberty by militant Islam? The sad but increasingly obvious fact is there is no such number. We are the frog in the pot of water, and the flame has been turned up. Why don't we feel it?

It has been said that if you drop a frog into scalding hot water, it will instantly hop out, but, if you place a frog in a pot of cool water, you can slowly heat the water and boil the frog alive without it ever noticing. I love the metaphor whether the science behind it holds up or not. The free world – America in particular – is that frog in the pot of water. The flames of militant Islam are steadily lapping at the pot, and all we feel is a cozy warmth. This is true even though the heating is no longer slow, but the flame has been turned up to high. Any real frog – even an incredibly dense one - would have hopped out of the pot long ago. We, on the other hand – the metaphorical frog – have been conditioned by our political and social cultures to believe that what we have been feeling for the last several years is not the flames being turned up but the addition of soothing jets. We are being cooked alive in the pot over a raging flame of militant

Islam while *we have deluded ourselves* into believing we are just relaxing at the spa, basking in the therapeutic heat of the jetted hot tub of political and social correctness. Our future is bleak indeed. Now, to understand our bleak future, we must understand militant Islam, and we must understand it's phenomenal rise in the face of the greatest military powers in the world.

First, we must denude militant Islam of the cloak of political correctness and false understanding that we have so willingly – indeed gleefully - draped it in. Militant Islam **is not a perversion of Islam**. I know it is fashionable to say it is, but that simply is not the case, and anyone with even a cursory education on Islam knows this. It is instead more accurately described as **radical fundamentalist Islam**. In fact, militant Islam is arguably in the eyes of many *more* true to the letter and the spirit of the Qu'ran and the Hadith than is any other part of that faith. *Yet we are prevented by geopolitical and geosocial correctness from acknowledging that fact.* The geopolitical and geosocial correctness we so piously but delusionally bathe ourselves in every single day necessitates that we label militant Islam as some grotesque and evil perversion of a peaceful and tolerant religion – a perversion that cannot be understood. This self-righteous, misinformed, and misguided political and social correctness is going to get us all killed. To understand how, lets look at the phenomenal rise of militant Islam.

Prior to 9/11, militant Islam only rarely made the

headlines. As far as the general public was concerned, militant Islam was contained to the Middle-East / Arab countries and Iran, which is Persian, by the way. We knew about the overthrow of the Shah in Iran and the holding of American hostages by adherents of militant Shiite Islam. We knew about the Arab-Israeli conflicts, Hezbollah, and the bombing of the Marine barracks in Beirut. We knew about the World Trade Center bombing and the embassy bombings in Kenya and Tanzania as well as some encounters with Iran in the Persian Gulf and the Strait of Hormuz (U.S. downing of Iranian "airliner"and re-flagging of Kuwaiti tankers). We knew about the attack on the U.S.S. Cole, but this handful of things is pretty much all the general public knew much about involving militant Islam.

Then the attacks of 9/11 happened. However, had the Pentagon not been hit and the World Trade Center towers not collapsed, the attacks would most likely have been viewed not as an act of war but as just another criminal act like the World Trade Center bombing and the embassy bombings in Kenya and Tanzania, which elicited only a few halfhearted cruise missile attacks in Afghanistan and Sudan. Instead, the attacks of 9/11 caused us to launch in earnest our war on terror. To be fair, though, many in positions of power still view the acts of 9/11 as criminal acts and not acts of war *per se*. Regardless, we have been in Afghanistan ever since, and if we leave completely, it will be in the hands of militant Islam before you can say "I told you so." Much ground has already been lost.

The Iraq War, which is often understandably conflated with the War on Terror, was conducted to enforce U.N. resolutions but eventually became, at least in part, a counterinsurgency war against militant Islam. With the U.S. pullout came chaos and the rapid rise of the Islamic State, which started out as Al Qaeda in Iraq then renamed itself the Islamic State of Iraq and Al Sham (ISIS), renamed itself again to the Islamic State of Iraq and the Levant (ISIL), and finally renamed itself (yet again) simply the Islamic State (IS) and declared a caliphate.

I do not mean to say, as some do, that, had the U.S. stayed in Iraq, there would be no Islamic State. It is entirely possible that the Islamic State would have risen up had the U.S. stayed. In fact, the presence of Al Qaeda in Iraq, the precursor organization to the Islamic State, was attributable directly to the U.S. presence there. U.S. presence in Iraq could possibly have slowed the advance of the Islamic State, though, had force been employed intelligently and expeditiously.

So, the U.S. fought two very long wars in Muslim lands, one of which continues today. After over 13 long years of fighting, militant Islam has grown *twenty-fold*. Until the Islamic State, Al Qaeda was not nor had it ever *truly* been on its heels, and "core Al Qaeda," if there even is or ever has been such a thing, had not been defeated. Al Qaeda is on the decline, though – and dramatically so – not because of anything we have done but because of the drain on funds and recruiting that is the much more charismatic and romantic Islamic State. As will be discussed later in this book, the war on terror has been an abject failure. That is inescapably true, unless of course, the objective was to ignite a firestorm of growth in militant Islam. If the object was to pile up dead bodies of Islamic militants in a manner which was *guaranteed* to introduce into the world a conflagration of hatred for the infidel West that cannot be effectively snuffed out by conventional means, then the war on terror has been an unmitigated and indeed stunning success.

Over the course of the war on terror, militant Islam has grown by an incredible 2000%. There are easily *20 times* as many Islamic militants now as there were on 9/11. Though some analysts put the figure as low as 500%, I am inclined to believe the 2000% figure given the information gathered by my advance teams in the Islamic State theater of operation, together with other information.

Though we did not intend to be the major factor in the growth of Militant Islam, we have indeed been the most direct and effective driver of its growth and its radicalization to the severe extreme. You will read this sentiment more than once in this book. Though our actions beginning with the Gulf War and continuing through the War on Terror and the Iraq war have been justified, they have also spurred the greatest growth militant Islam has ever seen. Unless and until we understand that the inexorable rise of militant Islam is a direct reaction to our actions, justified and just as they have been, we can have no hope of combating it. It is our failure to recognize this causal relationship that has allowed us to continue to project force in self-defense in such a way that is not only of little effect but is in fact counterproductive. (I will discuss the social mechanisms by which this happens later in this book.) It is our complete and utter inability to grasp this unfortunate and troublesome fact which dooms us.

The Internet / World Wide Web has been a major facilitator of radicalization. Were it not for the Crusades, the Gulf War, and the twin wars of the War on Terror and the Iraq War, we would certainly not see this level of radicalization and militarization in Islam, and we may not see any at all. However, those things have happened, and the War on Terror continues. Militant Islam is growing at a rate that should alarm even the most reserved doves among us. The stunning swiftness with which militant Islam is growing is owed solely to the Internet. The internet is not the cause of the radicalization at all. It is, as I say, a facilitator, and an extremely effective facilitator at that. No longer do people have to be associated with the right groups in the right places to be exposed to radical militant thinking and propaganda. They get it online. Through websites and social media, people are exposed to a world of militant Islamic indoctrination. The like-minded latch onto it and run with it and are bolstered by it. For others who may not have been exposed to it, it can seem new and exciting and glorious. For many, it turns out, this message of hate fills a void or a need in their lives. It is all bullshit, and any thinking person knows that, but the Islamic State are masters of the message. They know just how to appeal to specific, vulnerable groups of people, and they know just how to romanticize evil. This is the most charismatic and appealing a group of despicable, evil sons of bitches could ever be, and their job of recruiting and their quest for legitimacy are made exponentially easier by the Internet.

I want to take this opportunity to discuss another term I will never employ, because it has absolutely no legitimacy in the context of militant Islam: *lone wolf*. There is no such thing. A person committing a "lone wolf" attack may, in the most technical sense possible, be acting alone, but he is not acting in a vacuum. He may technically be a lone gunman, but he isn't truly acting alone. He is always acting in furtherance of militant Islam and at the behest of the radicalizers. Haven't they been urging attacks in the United States – especially on military soft targets? The "lone wolf" sees himself as part of the war, and so do those who radicalized him online.

This brings me to another term that has no legitimacy and is a total myth: *self-radicalized*. Truly self-radicalized people are few and far between, and they stand out. Think Charles Manson. Think Ted Kaczynski. The "lone wolf" who acts in furtherance of militant Islam may have indeed and probably has been radicalized online, but he is **not** self-radicalized. He has become radicalized through exposure to the message and likely through communication with some of the charismatic radicalizers who troll the Internet romanticizing and glorifying militant Islam and looking for recruits. Militant Islam radicalized him. He did not radicalize himself!

Other than the Internet, there is something else that has facilitated the rapid growth of militant Islam: our lack of will to fight it.

LACK OF WILL

U.S. Secretary of Defense Ash Carter has stated that recent advances by IS in Iraq are due not to the superior numbers of IS but to a lack of will to fight on the part of Iraqi forces who basically just ran away. In addition, only 60 Syrians have been trained to fight IS when the Department of Defense had expected to have 5400 trained by now, and the number of Iraqi forces showing up for training has been much lower than hoped for as well. These facts are not solely a testimony to the difficulty of getting Arabs to fight other Arabs (IS is slowly composed less and less of Arabs and more and more of foreign fighters) but also and possibly primarily to the effectiveness of IS terror. The terror is so effective that the will to resist IS has been, in most cases, reduced to a superficial will to fight that often evaporates in the face of the stark realities of actually engaging IS ans the consequences of capture. My men have witnessed it on more than one occasion

While Team Swandog advance teams were operating throughout the IS theater of operations for six full months completely undetected by IS - not to mention any of the world's greatest intelligence services – in numbers as high as 480, they encountered a few groups of locals who wanted desperately for my men to train them to execute hit and run attacks on both fixed and mobile IS targets. On three occasions, Team Swandog operators provided such training. When the first group executed their attack, not a single one of them actually fired at the enemy. They fired over their heads or into the air, the ground, or nearby buildings or automobiles. My men observed the operation but were not authorized to participate or come to the aid of the locals. After the botched guerrilla attack, which lasted all of 45 seconds, all of the locals involved were able to escape to a rendezvous point in a safe zone.

When my men asked them why they did what they did, it became apparent that they had lost their nerve. Although *in theory* they wanted to fight IS *very much*, in practice they lacked the courage and the will to face IS terror down. They were too afraid that, if the operation resulted in their capture, they would be tortured then beheaded or immolated on the Internet. They thought that, if they were captured, they could show their IS captors that they never really fired at them but instead made sure they missed, hoping IS would have mercy on them. IS terror is extremely effective – especially on the indigenous population. Their fear of being tortured and meeting a gruesome death on the internet or being cooked and fed to each other or their families successfully eroded their courage and will to fight

It was the same with the other two groups, except they never even attempted their attacks. One group finished their training, selected a target, and then chickened out at the last minute and disbanded. Only two of 46 even showed up at the rally point. When asked why, they said it was their fear of what would happen to them if they were captured. The other group refused to even select a target, claiming there simply was "no suitable target" in the entire IS theater of operation. There were indeed many – even lots in the immediate area. That group disbanded in shame within days. IS terror is working extremely well on most of the indigenous population, and they no longer have the will to fight and win.

Whether it is a result of the extreme terror of IS or of a shared Arab heritage or some combination of the two, the will to fight and destroy IS simply is not there. Watch some of the news footage of the Iraqis fighting. They clearly aren't willing to do what is necessary to fight and win. They always hide in a ditch and stick their AKs up and fire a wildly unaimed and uncontrolled volley in the general direction of the enemy and often into the air. Similarly, they hid behind walls and stick their AKs around the corner and fire, I presume praying that one of the rounds will even get close to the enemy. In my opinion, these people have no business fighting in a military force. Maybe they should be cooks or tailors or doctors or lawyers. They certainly don't have the will to fight the Islamic State effectively.

The Iraqis, though, are not the only ones who lack the will to do what is necessary to win. The rest of the world does as well. The West is very quick to say that IS in Iraq is an Iraqi problem and must have an Iraqi solution – just as quick as we are to say that IS in general is an Arab problem and that the solution must be an Arab one. Of course, all the while, we're willing to conduct a halfhearted bombing campaign (so we don't look like we're doing absolutely nothing) and simultaneously refuse to directly arm and train **the only indigenous forces with the will to do what is necessary to win – the Kurds**. I would love to give the Kurds elite training in guerrilla warfare, and I hope I get the chance to do someday. Right now the West is leaving these courageous and dedicated people twisting in the wind.

The West does not want to look disinterested, but we *certainly* don't have the will to do what is necessary to eliminate what is clearly not just an Iraqi problem or even just an Arab problem anymore but a *global* problem. We do the safe thing – bombing, and we only do that halfheartedly *at best*. This is not the fault of the brave men and women of our armed forces. It is squarely on the politicians and on the people who elect them. It is *our* fault. We have bought in to the institutionalized idiocy, and the result has been a twenty-fold increase in militant Islam and an ever-increasing perceived geosocial and geopolitical legitimacy of their terrible ideology. The greater their perceived legitimacy, the harder it is to rally support against them.

A LOOK AHEAD

Militant Islam aims to take over the world. **Make no mistake about it.** The goal of militant Islam is to subjugate *the entire world* to their brand of Islam and Sharia law, because *they believe they have been commanded by Allah and Muhammad to do so.* They are actively pursuing this goal, and we are not even close to taking this as seriously as we should. We dismiss the very notion as absurd and laugh it off when instead we should be afraid. We shouldn't be hysterical, but we should have a healthy, sober fear of a movement which is gaining steam at a phenomenal rate and which fully intends to see us either converted to their brand of Islam, subjugated to it and paying the jizyah ... or dead.

Do you see how the Islamic State treats people? Do you know even a few of the horror stories coming out of Iraq and Syria? It is not the purpose of this book to recount them all here, and to do so would more than double its volume. I will, however, remind the reader that life under militant Islam would be pure Hell for a freedom-loving people. Once they are in charge here, homosexuals will be executed in very brutal ways as people are in Iraq and Syria every day even on the barest suspicion of homosexuality. They stage mass executions of Christians over there, and they will do so here. They take extreme joy in beheading people over there, and they will take even more joy in it here in the land of the homeland of the infidel. If you oppose the caliphate, you and your whole family may be burned alive and the video distributed on the Internet. They executed one young man, cooked him, and fed him to his mother when she came looking for him. We can expect more of the same and even worse here. Is this the kind of regime you want to live under and pay jizyah to?

They will bring violence to the modern West on a large scale. It is in their plan and within their *current* capabilities. I'm not even really sure what they're waiting on. Their jihad gives them license to kill in the most barbaric fashion. Once they take over, we will either have to convert to their brand of Islam, agree to accept second-class status in their vision of a Muslim world and pay the jizyah, or be executed. Sound fun to you? Even if you don't convert and instead accept second-class status and pay jizyah, any time they decide you're making mischief in the land, they can kill you. They will probably do so in some grotesque and very public fashion. The party just keeps getting better. This is what we have to look forward to.

Gone will be the freedom of religion. The freedom of

speech will meet the same fate as will all the other freedoms we have grown accustomed to. There will be no more innocent until proven guilty. Modernity will be deemed sinful, education taboo. We will live in constant fear of arbitrary execution. No more free world as we know it. Most of what we watch on TV and view on the Internet will be deemed sinful and banned. The new Internet porn will be video after video of beheadings and immolations and other savage executions of infidels. Ah, but this is at the end of the war, though. There is an ugly struggle through which we must first come, and by the time it is over, there will not likely be much left.

      The free world as we know it will most likely be turned to rubble in this struggle. I'm sure you've seen the shape of cities we have liberated. They are largely flattened. We will turn our own world to a smoldering heap of rubble in this war because we will keep trying to defeat this very unconventional enemy by very conventional means. Because we are infected with the psychosis of institutionalized idiocy, we are unable as a nation-state and as a culture to learn and to adapt at a pace that will save us. Our unfounded but ardent and sincere belief that the vast superiority of our fighting force – our war machine – will carry the day will be our undoing. Did it carry the day in Vietnam? Why should we believe it would do so now against a much more ruthless, determined, and better-funded foe? If the might of the American war machine could not prevail against an unconventional enemy fighting for its political and cultural ideology, what basis is there to think that it would prevail against an even more unconventional enemy fighting for its religious ideology - *for its god*? After 13 years in Afghanistan, militant Islam is is strong there as it ever was. Are you getting the picture, here?

So, basically, we will keep doing the same thing that hasn't worked for us for the last 13+ years. Why? Because that's what we do. Ever since we won WWII in such fashion that it was clear we were not a country to be fucked with, we never fight the war we are in but instead we fight some other war from our history. The Gulf War is an arguable exception. What do the Iraq war and the War on Terror have in common? We have fought both as conventional wars. To the extent that the War on Terror continues, we are still fighting it as a conventional war. That is why we are losing. Later in this book I will show in humiliating fashion how our institutionalized idiocy has been losing the War on Terror for us from day one. **We are not fighting the war we are in!**

Now, I know there will be an uproar of military families and pro-military politicians and others who will raise the cry that we are winning the war on Terror and will be able to cite all kinds of numbers as to how many of the enemy we have killed and how many of their leaders we have taken out with drone strikes and so on and so forth. Yes, I know we killed Bin Laden. I am not saying that our men and women in the military are not the best there is. They certainly are. I am not saying that they are not doing their duty in the most admirable and amazing fashion. They certainly are. What I am saying is that the figures relied upon to find success in the War on Terror have nothing whatsoever to do with success in this type of war. This war is unlike any other in which we have been engaged. We must therefore fight it like no other war we have ever fought. The true measure of success – the only true measure – is the extent in both numbers and territory of militant Islam. By that measure, our War on Terror has been and continues to be a dismal and humiliating failure. Militant Islam measures today 20 times what it did on 9/11. I will show you exactly why in later chapters.

Let me pause to give credit where credit is due. The initial phase of the Iraq war was a stunning success. It was so because it was a conventional war against a conventional enemy. In such a head-to-head fight there is no power on the planet that could dream of standing up to the United States and the other powers of the modern West. None. We have superior everything including training and morale. If the War on Terror had been a conventional war and we had been fighting a conventional enemy, we would have had the thing wrapped up in less than a year. This has never, though, been a conventional war, and we have never in this war faced a conventional enemy. The great shame is that we have never fought it and never will fight it as the war it really is.

We will instead continue to the bitter end fighting it *as the war we wish it was.*

Knowing that we will keep doing the same thing that has for the last 13+ years been losing us this war, what hope is there that we would be able to prevail just because the fighting comes to the shores of America and the modern West? None. We will *not* prevail. We will be defeated, and we will destroy our infrastructure in the process of the defeat, because that is all we know how to do anymore. The saddest part is we will in the end be left scratching our heads trying to figure out why we lost.

I know what you're thinking, but you're only half right. America is an armed free country, and no invading army would stand a chance on our ground. The People would rise up and drive the invading army out. That is true of any conventional army and any conventional invasion conceivable. Russia will never invade the United States, and neither will China. It doesn't matter how big their armies are. No nation-state and no conventional army in the world could hope in its grandest of delusions to succeed in military action on our soil. **They would be laid waste by the armed citizen.**

Unfortunately, that is not the case with militant Islam. Militant Islam is not a traditional nation-state and has about the farthest thing from a conventional military that one can imagine. Militant Islam is a hodgepodge of closely related religious ideologies each seeking world domination. Their political ideologies are a part of *and subordinate to* their religious ideologies. The fighting forces of these different groups are extremely unconventional, and therein lies the rub. The war on our soil will not be a conventional invasion by a conventional armed force. The invasion has been quietly taking place under our noses for decades. Because we have freedom of religion, *which we must*, and because we want to be as inclusive as possible, we have been allowing the enemy to lawfully move to America – welcoming them, even The truth is we have no idea how many of the Muslims in our own country are truly moderate and how many subscribe to a militant ideology. We have no idea how many who have immigrated here or were perhaps even born here who are now being radicalized online. There is no invasion in the traditional sense for our military or our armed citizenry to resist.

There will also be no front. The enemy's strategy is to attrit and terrorize us into submission and subjugation. The battles in this war will all be things there is no way for a free society to defend against. They will shoot up or blow up our shopping malls and concerts and festivals and movie theaters and churches and kill and terrorize us in dozens of other similar ways. America and the modern West are chock full of soft targets, and these are targets that cannot be hardened and the People remain free. These "battles" I am talking about will all be won before we even have a chance to engage, whether it is the military or the armed citizens doing the engaging. There will be countless such battles. The perpetrators of such attacks will either become martyrs or will melt back into our open and diverse culture by the time we have a chance to get organized. Graphic videos of these "battles" will play out on the Internet. Citizens who are captured will be beheaded or immolated or murdered in some other gruesome fashion online for the rest of the country and the world to see. We will be killed off, and we will be terrorized, and we will have no way to effectively defend against it. We could try to purge the land of all Muslims, but that would harm and alienate the moderates, and it also assumes we would be able to distinguish the militants from the moderates. They are not the type to wear armbands like the Jews did for Hitler. This is all just a terrible fact of how the war in which we are engaged is going to go when it reaches our homeland.

Our military trains in counterinsurgency, but not to a great degree, and we are not going to be dealing with the average, run-of-the-mill insurgency here. The fact is there is no way to train for a war like the one that is coming, and there is no way to win such a war and stay free. The only hope would be found in absolutely locking everything down. This would kill our economy and turn our country into a totalitarian military dictatorship. None of us want that. I guess we could just go around killing anyone who "looks Islamic," but that would mean a lot of innocent people would die at our hands, and really, can we tell a Muslim from a

non-Muslim anymore? The militants are recruiting more
and more people who do not have the traditional Middle-
Eastern look. It simply isn't doable. Even if it was, it would
mean the absolute rejection of the core values shared by all
people in the modern West.

The armed citizenry would be of even less effect than
the military would be. This is true first because the citizenry
has little to no training on how to deal with such an enemy
and second *because we do not have an effectively armed
citizenry.* Our culture has developed a neurotic and quite
absurd discomfort with the carrying of weapons – especially
openly carrying them. We own guns, but almost none of us
carry them. Most of us who carry them carry them
concealed. You can't fight the enemy who is shooting up the
shopping mall you are in when your gun is at home. Also,
the enemy isn't going to look at you and know you have a gun
at home and therefore decide not to shoot up the mall or
theater or church you are in. He might, on the other hand,
see a good number of people with pistols on their hips and
the occasional long gun over their shoulder and decide to
forego his "battle" against those armed infidels. More on this
in the next chapter.

One thing you are going to see when this war comes to
our soil is the rise of vigilante militias. Citizens motivated by
the most sincere patriotism will band together and hunt
down anyone they think is a militant Muslim. It *is* going to
get ugly – very ugly. There is no escaping it. They will be

everywhere, and they will kill a lot of innocent people, but they will be small, and they will be the minority. Most citizens will not be able to figure out what to do. The rest will simply be too terrorized to act. I know the extreme terror has worked very well in the Middle-East, and I have every reason to believe it would work just as well in America and the modern West. Why? Because we are all humans, and we have, for the most part, the same psychology. Extreme terror works. Extreme terror is extremely effective at destroying the will to resist. More on this in the next chapter.

The outlook is indeed quite bleak. We do far more to appease and even enable militant Islam and to increase its legitimacy in the world than we do to combat it and to undermine its legitimacy. We purposefully – indeed gleefully – blind ourselves to the defining qualities of our enemy when doing so forecloses any possibility of defeating them. We are only capable of developing conventional strategies to fight this unconventional enemy, and these are strategies which may kill many radicals but end up creating far more than they kill. We have pussified our culture to the point that the sight of anyone other than a police officer carrying a weapon sends us into hysteria, so we no longer have an effectively armed citizenry capable of defending itself against the kinds of attacks we will be subjected to in the coming phase of this war. Furthermore, any war against this enemy on our soil would result in the decimation of our infrastructure and cannot be won without the abandonment of many of our core principles, the reign of total chaos, and the rise of a totalitarian military dictatorship and vigilante militias roaming about and killing anyone suspected of being Islamic.

There is a way out, though. This can be prevented. We don't *have* to be doomed. We can change our future, but to do so, we're going to have to grow a fucking pair – a pair of qualities that are absolutely essential to dragging ourselves up out of the mire of institutionalized idiocy and standing up to the extreme terror which will be visited on us. Those qualities are a courageous character and the capacity for creativity and unconventional thought.

2
Institutionalized Idiocy and Extreme Terror

The primary factors in the coming fall of the United States and the modern West to militant Islam are institutionalized idiocy and extreme terror. I talk about the fall of America and the rest of the modern West to militant Islam like it is a foregone conclusion because, **unless we change our way of thinking radically and quickly**, it *is* a foregone conclusion. We certainly can't hope to defeat the Islamic State, much less eradicate militant Islam as a whole, thinking the way we are. Let's take a closer look at the institutionalized idiocy and the extreme terror which will be our undoing if we don't soon get a grip.

THE IDIOCY

Let's look first at the institutionalized idiocy that now dooms us and which we must shake off if we are to have hope of the continuation of the free world. It takes a lot of forms including the enshrinement of geopolitical and geosocial correctness in our culture and the weaving of that carcinogenic thread into the very fabric of our society. It also takes the form of arrogance – the belief that we are invincible. It takes the form of a belief that we can do more with less and the corresponding downsizing of our military, and it takes the form of always training to fight a war other than the one that is on the horizon. In addition, it takes the form of anti-gun hysteria in our own country.

We wear our institutionalized idiocy like a badge of honor when we should be wearing it as a mark of shame and humiliation – a scarlet letter, if you will. We think it is a good thing that we are trying to win the world's respect by denouncing our hegemony and publicly ridiculing the notion of a hegemony of America and the modern West. We think it makes us more sensitive and therefore better people if we see only the good in people and turn a blind eye to the bad that threatens our very existence. We think it makes us better people to try to negotiate with those with whom there *obviously is no negotiation* and to trust those who *obviously cannot be trusted*. We think it makes us enlightened people to ignore and even deny the Islamic nature of militant Islam. We think that the power of our conventional war machine will prevail against any enemy, and we assume every enemy has a normal, healthy, ordered world view. We therefore have no ability to formulate a strategy that takes into account the neuroses which drive our enemies, and we have only a vestigial ability to engage in unconventional warfare and develop unconventional strategies or tactics. We think it makes us a more civilized people if we leave our guns at home and relegate the notion of the armed citizen to the days of the "wild west." We are wrong on every count. We couldn't be more wrong.

Geopolitical and Geosocial Correctness

It's natural to want to be loved. Don't we all want to be loved? I know I do. Yet cultures and nation-states are not people. They are collectives. It is good for a culture or a nation-state to be loved, but there are times when it is far better for a culture or nation-state to be respected and feared. Is it better for a country to pussify itself in order to be loved and seen as civilized by all (except its enemies, which will always hate it) or to be strong and resolute and uncompromising in its national defense in order to be respected by all and feared by its enemies? What do you think? If you are a liberal Obama/Clinton acolyte, you probably think the former is the path to greatness and the latter is the path to destruction. If you instead have a fully functional brain in your head, you realize that it is far better to be respected and feared than to be loved. Of course, you can be loved, respected, and feared by all the right people simultaneously as was the case for the United States from WWII to the turn of the millennium.

Look at us now. In our quest to be loved by all, we are

feared by few, trusted by fewer still, and respected by none. Even our allies are making deals with our geopolitical enemies. (Just look at Saudi Arabia making its nuke deal with Russia, for crying out loud!) When I say *we*, I am, as an American, talking primarily about America, but I am also talking to a great extent about the modern West, which has hopped on board this crazy train right along with us. All the countries of the modern West want to be seen as civilized and open and tolerant and welcoming and accepting of all cultures and religions. We would rather be seen in the eyes of the world as *anything* but bigots. There seems to be a competition to see which modern Western country can be the most adamant that Islam is a peaceful and tolerant religion and the most ignorant of the Islamic nature of militant Islam. In this competition, we will hand militant Islam the keys to the front door. Many would argue that we already have. They may well be right.

We want to avoid, **at all costs no matter how great**, being seen as colonial powers seeking to gain territory or expand our sphere of control. Colonialism or imperialism simply isn't hip like it used to be, so we want to be above even the most strained and absurd accusations of colonialism. Therefore, we apologize for merely perceived colonialism or imperialism on our part, and we adapt our behavior and cripple our national defense in an effort to avoid the label of colonialism. I can think of a lot worse things than colonialism, **like being subjugated under**

militant Islam and paying jizyah to these assholes.

We are gradually committing suicide by way of the poison pill of geosocial and geopolitical correctness. We deny the harsh realities of this world in the name of civilization. In the name of civilization, we welcome into our country with open arms the barbarian hoards who would destroy us. We are so far above the concept of religious war that we would rather gouge out our own eyes than see the truth that we *are* in a religious war. We are not in it by our own choosing, but we *are* in it. We are not in it to win it, though, and we never will be ... unless we quickly and radically alter our way of thinking.

There's more to our collective madness. We are leaving Israel out in the cold while cozying up with Iran on the bear skin rug in front of the fireplace with a nice bottle of Asti. This kind of madness first presented back when, after a great job by our military in Afghanistan, we allowed the country to reconstitute itself as the Islamic Republic of Afghanistan instead of insisting on a secular government like we damn well should have. How stupid was that? Now we are courting the Islamic Republic of Iran – one of the largest bastions of militant Islam and one of the largest state sponsors of terrorism. We brought Israel to the prom, but now we're playing tonsil hockey with Iran right in front of her. Guess which one we want to fool around in the back seat with now. We're just too stupid to see our new prom date is a black widow.

I hear a lot of people calling Obama a Muslim and putting it all on him, and that's not fair. Though he acts like he wants to hand the world over to militant Islam, it's not just Obama. Not by a long shot. There are many who are right there with him. We could name Biden and Kerry and Clinton just for starters. It's not just America either. Five other countries have been involved in the quadruple overtime negotiations with Iran as well. Iran has more suitors than a porn star on a dating site. Why? Institutionalized idiocy. We have to deny the truths about Iran and militant Islam and be seen as accepting of and cooperative with those different than us – especially militant Islam for some reason. It is just fashionable in this world to deny the true nature of the enemy and to treat as friends those who chant for our death in the public square. It's just fucking insane!

Look at the deal our President has gotten us into with Iran. Iran was under some pretty tough sanctions designed to keep them from getting a nuclear weapon. They were illegally working toward one anyway, so instead of ramping up the sanctions in order to keep a state sponsor of terrorism who calls us the "Great Satan" and wants little more than to see us gone from getting a nuclear weapon, we got the absolutely brilliant idea of removing some of the sanctions *just to get them to talk with us on the nuke issue*. Then we let deadline after deadline pass as the talks went into quadruple overtime. I wonder if we know the meaning of the word deadline. Dictionary.com defines it as "the time by which something must be finished or submitted; the latest time for finishing something" or alternatively as "a line or limit that must not be passed." Maybe it's the word *must* that we don't get the meaning of. Truth be told, there never was an actual deadline. We were so hell-bent on getting a deal – even a bad deal – that we were going to swap spit in the shower with Iran until we got it, no matter how many "deadlines" we had to blow through or how much of the free world's safety we had to give up to get it.

Not only did we pass "deadline" after "deadline," but we got a deal which does not guarantee any of the requirements we started out with. We are trusting a regime which quite obviously cannot be trusted. We are trusting a regime which stages demonstrations at which "death to Israel" and "death to America" are chanted. It isn't trust but verify, either. It's trust and make an utterly meaningless and ineffectual pretense of verification. We built cheating right into the deal by saying all inspections the only meaningful sites to inspect must be noticed and giving Iran time to object then taking more time to arbitrate any disagreement over the inspection. Since Iran has already passed legislation forbidding the inspection of military sites, we'll see how well that goes. There is no meaningful verification of compliance in this deal. We schedule an inspection of an undeclared military nuke site we find out about, and they object to the inspection, buying time to hide all their contraband. Even if, after arbitration, we are allowed, there will be nothing there when we get there. All the while, Iran will be building a nuclear arsenal right under our idiotic noses.

Even worse, we are allowing Iran to work toward an ICBM. How stupid is that? Has the world truly gone insane? We also give them forever to reduce their stockpiles of fissile material. I cannot see how anybody with a handful of brain cells still talking to each other could see this as a good deal. It is the flagship product of institutionalized idiocy. We are on a course toward handing militant Islam the keys to the world – the means of our destruction and the destruction of everything we stand for, and we are patting ourselves on the back for it! Anyone who had anything to do with this deal should be locked in a padded room, chained to the floor, and force-fed anti-psychotic meds until they can see reality and are no longer a danger to the free world.

This isn't a book about everything that is wrong with Obama's precious legacy-making agreement. If it was, it would have to be ten times as long as it already is. I did, though, want the reader to understand some of the most glaring and egregious deficiencies so that the lengths to which we are willing to go and the danger in which we are willing to put ourselves and the free world into in the name of geopolitical and geosocial correctness **and in the name of one leader's legacy** can be fully understood.

I know Congress has 60 days to review and sign off on the deal, but Emperor Obama has already said he will veto the Congress' "veto" of his precious, legacy-making deal should it happen, and I know the numbers are not there to override his veto. There are simply too many in Congress who are drunk on the powerful spirit of institutionalized idiocy and eaten up with the dumbass to boot. I could be wrong, but I think the chance that Congress will nix this horrible deal which basically hands Iran everything we say we don't want them to have is smaller than the chance of an August blizzard in Miami. The smart money is on institutionalized idiocy.

That's all moot, anyway, because Emperor Barack Hussein Obama the Great got the horrible Iran nuke deal, which is nothing more than a wink and a nod to Iran's clandestine development of nuclear weapons, done as a U.N Resolution, thereby bypassing Congress and making any debate in or vote by Congress completely academic. Sometimes his actions seem not only completely disdainful of our system of government but *calculated* to bring about our demise at the hands of militant Islam.

We were so bent on getting this deal that we hung at least three and possibly four Americans being held in captivity in Iran out to dry. We could have made their release a part of any deal, and God knows we should have, but we didn't . For some reason that is completely fucking insane, we found it more important to negotiate a deal that we can say keeps Iran from getting a nuclear weapon but in actuality does nothing. We could have accomplished what we claim we want to accomplish with a few more sanctions and, if necessary, a clandestine operation or two. Instead, we had to demonstrate what civilized and accepting and blindly trusting Islamophiles we are by negotiating a horrible deal. At every step, we have made unacceptable concessions. If you want to know who got the better end of the deal, just look at who was smiling more afterward. Iran got its happy ending, and all we got was a bitter taste in our mouths.

Did anybody catch the Chamberlainesque peace in our time speeches by John Kerry and the Idiot-in-Chief after the deal was reached. Those speeches literally made me nauseated. I seriously almost threw up. That isn't hyperbole or exaggeration. I was sick. Does anybody study history anymore? Anybody? These guys are going to come off like the biggest clowns in history – yes, even bigger than Neville Chamberlain. Anyone who thinks this is a good deal is simply stupid in the extreme. This deal is just one more chapter in the story of our own downfall. Our foreign policy is not the only aspect of our institutionalized idiocy, though.

Lack of Imagination, Adaptability, and the Capacity for Unconventional Thought

9/11 has been said to be the result of a failure of imagination. I believe it. We simply have no imagination anymore. Not only are we unable to think of even a tiny fraction of the ways in which our enemy will attack us, but we are also unable to imagine new ways of approaching the problem. We keep doing the same thing over and over again and always expecting a different result, and we shoot down imaginative solutions without even evaluating them, because imagination is no longer welcome. We feel threatened by the new and innovative.

Another but related aspect of our institutionalized idiocy is our worship of conformity and the conventional. New and innovative ideas are only valued in the business world, it seems. Just look at how the worlds of politics and of political and social correctness treat ideas which do not conform to their prevailing world views. Watch how this book is received in those worlds. **Why are we so afraid of creative and unconventional thought?** Are we afraid someone may be smarter than we are? Why are we so invested in a world view, a foreign policy, and a war strategy that are clearly handing our enemies the means with which to destroy us?

We are clearly incapable of realizing the type of war we are in and adapting our tactics to win it. As I have stated, we have been fighting an unconventional enemy with a conventional strategy and conventional tactics for over 13 years. The result is that we have killed our fair share of radicals, but militant Islam is now 20 times stronger than it was on 9/11. Still, I am one of only a very few out there screaming for us to change our strategy and tactics. Everyone else just wants either more or less of the same things that have been so counterproductive for the length of this war. I guess there is nobody in public office or in the command structure of the military and intelligence community that has the capacity for free and unconventional thought.

Anyone with a brain can see that our conventional war is not working. It hasn't been working for 13 years, and it's not going to just magically start working because we want it to or because we have a nuke deal with Iran or because we are downsizing our military and trying to become a kinder, gentler nation. We are intransigent in our conventional strategy and tactics, and our intransigence is loosing the war for us.

Related to this is our arrogance. We think we are invincible and that our military can handle any task, regardless of how unconventional the enemy. We also are so far gone into the belief of the infallibility of our decisions that we stick to them even when they are clearly not working. An example of this would be the shift to SIGINT (signals intelligence) and away from HUMINT (human intelligence). We have deluded ourselves into thinking our technology and methods are so awesome that SIGINT is all that is needed. We feel we can gain all the intelligence we need via SIGINT. This is why we are having so much trouble finding targets to bomb in the Islamic State theater of operation. We know we are having troubles due to lack of HUMINT, but are we even considering beefing up our HUMINT capabilities? No. Instead we seek to compensate for lack of HUMINT by adding more SIGINT and by doing stupid and unconstitutional things like spying on Americans. All you Obama haters out there need to know that this is not exclusively an Obama thing. Bush had just as much and maybe more to do with it.

Our lack of imagination, adaptability, and the capacity for unconventional thought are like a tumor with tentacles reaching all throughout and infecting all of our institutions, but there is more to our institutionalized idiocy than that. There's our anti-gun hysteria. This trend away from the carrying of guns has placed our society in grave danger.

Anti-Gun Hysteria

There was a time in this country when men used to carry guns. Some had one on each hip. It was a normal everyday sight, and nobody gave a man carrying a gun or two a second thought unless he was brandishing it, robbing the place, or shooting the place up. We have since fallen under the insane and utterly unsupported delusion that it is inherently dangerous for law-abiding citizens to carry guns in public. Contrary to evidence and common sense, we believe that having law-abiding citizens disarmed in public somehow reduces violent crime. It doesn't. Just compare states with traditional open carry like Vermont to states like Illinois and even my home state of Arkansas, which has not traditionally been open carry. Which have the highest rates of violent crime? You guessed it ... those with the most gun restrictions. The wild west wasn't dangerous because law-abiding citizens carried guns. Law-abiding citizens carried guns because the wild west was a dangerous place. America and the countries of the modern West will all be very dangerous places when the Islamic militants bring their war to us, **which they will**.

We have replaced a healthy fear of man with an irrational fear of the gun. It isn't the human being, capable of all manner of violent and evil thoughts as he is, that should be feared. It is the inanimate object which in and of itself is capable of no harm or ill will that should be feared. That is ridiculously fucked up. Equally fucked up is the idea that making something illegal will keep a criminal from doing it. We prohibit the carrying of weapons in an effort to make our public spaces safer, but all that accomplishes is eliminating the law-abiding citizen's ability to defend himself and other law-abiding citizens from the criminal with the gun – or the terrorist or Islamic State douchebag.

The idea that we are safer when law-abiding citizens do not carry guns has become an institution in this country – so much so that when the pendulum started to swing back toward citizen carry, it was *concealed* carry that was preferred. Why? Because of our institutionalized idiotic fear of *seeing* weapons in public. We are not over that fear yet. We are moving that direction as a culture, but slowly. Much too slowly. The anti-gun dipsticks will argue that having more guns in public does not make our public spaces safer but obviously makes them more dangerous. This argument is fatally flawed, because it views the gun as inherently dangerous rather than the person carrying it. Guns are not dangerous or evil, but people can be.

Due to our irrational anti-gun hysteria in this country, very few people other than law enforcement officers carry guns every day in public. This sad situation means we are unable to stop mass shootings and terrorist attacks. We will be able to defend against the tactics of the Islamic militants much more effectively if law-abiding citizens carry guns. I guess the anti-gun dipsticks would rather the Islamic Militants be able to walk into a crowded restaurant or church and be able to kill to their hearts content rather than to be subjected to the horror of having to see those evil guns carried by law-abiding citizens in public. We need to quickly regain our comfort with guns and accept the open carrying of guns everywhere an attack may occur. **The gun in your home does not protect you from the IS bastard shooting up the restaurant you are in, and the gun hidden under your shirt or in your purse does not deter him.** As this war enters its next phase where the hostilities are carried out on our soil, the utility of open carry will quickly become evident to any thinking person.

This is not an anti-gun control book or a pro Second Amendment book. I am leaving those arguments to others with much more time on their hands to write many more pages. I just want the reader to be able to see how anti-gun hysteria and our acquired cultural fear of guns and of law-abiding citizens being armed in public puts us all in danger from attacks by this enemy who doesn't give a rat's ass about our sissy laws.

THE TERROR

The Islamic State are masters of the use of extreme terror. Everyone else is the JV. I have seen the effects IS's use of extreme terror have had in the IS theater of operations, and it is almost paralyzing. Remember the groups my advance teams trained to engage in guerrilla warfare style attacks against IS? They are prime examples of the effectiveness of extreme terror. The effectiveness of extreme terror is a major reason why we only have 60 Syrians trained and a few hundred to a couple thousand Iraqis depending on where you get your information. Their use of extreme terror has been and will continue to be the key to their success – even when they are fighting us on our soil. I know we all want to think of ourselves as brave – this is the home of the brave, after all – but we are all going to be scared shitless when they start beheading us for show in our town squares and on the Internet and burning us alive for the world to see and cooking us and feeding us to each other. It takes an extremely special kind of person to overcome that fear and act in the face of the possibility of suffering the same fate.

Fear of death is one thing. Fear of torturous death like those we see in Islamic State recruiting videos is another thing entirely. Most people can overcome the simple fear of death. Our men and women in the military do it every day. I think we all have the capacity to overcome fear of death in combat. Unlike our enemy, none of us *want* to die, but the general idea of dying fighting for your home and your country and your family and your way of life and your god is not so fearsome that the average person cannot overcome the fear and act. Many of us could even romanticize the idea. I think few of us, though, could overcome the fear of a horrendous death – especially a torturous one. I have seen hardened special operators paralyzed by that fear.

We are all human, and there is nothing to be ashamed of in being paralyzed by the type of extreme terror IS brings. It is a natural human reaction, and there aren't too many of us that can get past it or have it trained out of us. That's one reason I don't expect a great uprising of armed citizens when the enemy brings that terror to our homeland. Given the choice of the safety we will have convinced ourselves hiding out brings or confronting an enemy who not only is not afraid to die but *wants* to die and who wants to subject us to the most horrible public torture and death, the vast, vast majority of us would choose hiding out. Given the choice of surrender and subjugation or fighting when there is the chance of capture and horrible, torturous public death, many of us would choose surrender. Perhaps a majority. Most of us would only fight when it was our only way out and our own death was certain unless we fought. It's what Sun Tzu refers to as death ground. By the time we reach death ground in our own homeland, it will be too late, and we won't have the numbers to effect the outcome.

Again, we all want to think of ourselves as brave and as heroes, but for the vast majority of us, the only fighting we will be doing is in our daydreams of glory. You can criticize me all you want, but I know people, and this is just a fact of humanity. Research and human history bear me out. This is why we need to kill them all over there before they start killing us all over here.

Between the institutionalized idiocy and the extreme terror, we are doomed to a future of subjugation to militant Islam, and Sharia law as they interpret it. I have said that we can change our future if we change our way of thinking quickly and radically. I know that is **impossible** for us to do as a culture and as a country. There is too much inertia to overcome. Our only hope is for a few of us who have the capacity for creativity and unconventional thought to find the workaround. We can change our future if we can find the right people with creativity and courage and the capacity for unconventional thought. It's going to have to be a few of us, but a few is all it's going to take. There is a way we can escape the institutionalized idiocy, avoid the extreme terror, and save the free world from the inexorable march of militant Islam. It starts with understanding our enemy, it continues with understanding that the War on Terror has been an abject failure *and understanding why* then understanding the quagmire that is the situation on the ground. It ends with the formulation of the correct strategy and tactics and putting that strategy and those tactics to relentless action until we have eradicated militant Islam from the planet.

3
Neuroses: The Social Mechanisms Behind the Rise of Militant Islam

IT'S THE CRUSADES, STUPID!

I know a lot of people are tired of hearing the geopolitically and geosocially correct politicians blaming the Crusades for militant Islam. Well, suck it up, and maybe you can make it through this chapter, because I am going to blame the Crusades. Actually, I'm not. I'm going to blame a neurotic culture which arose in the Arab-Islamic world as a reaction to the crusades, although the subtle difference is lost on most conformist political and social thinkers.

I am definitely *not blaming Christianity* for the rise of militant Islam, and I am most certainly *not justifying the atrocities* of militant Islam. Far from it. Christianity is not to blame, and the atrocities of militant Islam can never be justified. The rise of militant Islam and the spread of its violent ideology of terroristic jihad must, however, be explained. The explanation lies not in post-9/11 theorizing about the drivers of radicalization. That is the wrong rabbit hole to head down. None of those explanations hold up under critical analysis.

Whether you blame the Crusades and Christianity or American imperialism or the weakening of America's military or the economic stresses and disaffected youth in the Arab-Islamic world or the Obama-led rush toward disinvolvement in the world and rejection of the hegemony of America and the modern West, you have nothing solid to go on. All you have is hunch, emotion, and sociopolitical inclination. Every single post-9/11 attempt at explaining radicalization that I have seen is filtered through the lens of sociopolitical inclination. The more liberal the person advancing the attempted explanation, the more likely it is to blame the Crusades, Christianity, American imperialism, or the economic stresses and disaffected youth in the Arab-Islamic world. The more likely it is to ignore the cultural neuroses which pervade much of Arab-Islamic culture. The more conservative the person offering the supposed explanation, the more likely it is to blame the Obama-led stampede away from the hegemony of America and the modern West. The more likely it is to ignore the fact that the actions of America and the modern West play into the aforementioned cultural neuroses and indirectly and inadvertently drive radicalization.

To truly understand the drivers of radicalization and the rise of militant Islam, we must go to pre-9/11 analysis, which is far, far less likely to be warped by the crazy coke bottle lens of sociopolitical inclination. The problem is, that analysis is scant, and it almost always comes from a modern Western point of view. There is, however, an excellent Arab-Islamic point of view explanation provided in one short paragraph of a book not well-known outside of academia.

In my studies of Islam and the Arab-Islamic world, I read *The Crusades Through Arab Eyes* by Amin Maalouf. In the final paragraph of his epilogue, Maalouf provides the most elegant and pristine explanation for radicalization and jihad I have ever come across. His insight is also the most psychologically and sociologically sound. Though Maalouf doesn't label it as such, he describes in a few salient sentences what is in fact a cultural neurosis in a great part of the Arab-Islamic world where any action by the West is seen as a continuation of the Crusades, thereby justifying jihad. Here's the way Maalouf put it:

> In a Muslim world under constant attack, it is impossible to prevent the emergence of a sense of persecution, which among certain fanatics takes the form of a dangerous obsession. The Turk Mehmet Ali Agca, who tried to shoot the pope on 13 May 1981, had expressed himself in a letter in these terms: *I have decided to kill John Paul II,*

supreme commander of the Crusades. Beyond this individual act, it seems clear that the Arab East still sees the West as a natural enemy. Against that enemy, any hostile action – be it political, military, or based on oil – is considered no more than legitimate vengeance. And there can be no doubt that the schism between these two worlds dates from the Crusades, deeply felt by the Arabs, even today, as an act of rape.

At the time Maalouf wrote his book, a significantly smaller portion of the Arab-Islamic world was possessed of this neurosis than is now the case. It is now spreading like wildfire and is feeding on itself and the just but misguided post-9/11 actions by America and the modern West.

No, I am not hopping on the blame America, blame Christianity bandwagon. Not hardly. I am, however, an educated and open-minded realist who can see that militant Islam is a monster of our own creation. Did we intend to create this monster? No. Are we an imperialist power that has abused its hegemony? No, *but we are viewed as such* by a great and growing portion of the Arab-Islamic world due to the cultural neuroses at work in that population. Have our actions in Afghanistan, Iraq, and the rest of the Muslim world since 9/11 been just and justified? The overwhelming majority have been, but they have also been based on false assumptions about the world and about the ability of a conventional war to defeat the enemy and in a complete ignorance of the effect our actions would have in the Arab-

Islamic world.

We didn't intend to spur the greatest period of growth militant Islam has ever seen, but we did. We didn't intend to be the greatest driver of radicalization, but we have been. We were absolutely entitled to defend ourselves against Al Qaeda after 9/11, and we were completely justified in doing so. The fact that we have been 100% justified does not somehow magically cure the cultural neuroses at work in the Arab-Islamic world. There is nothing magical about America's war on terror, and the fact that our actions have been overwhelmingly just and justified does not mean they have not inadvertently caused this phenomenal rise of militant Islam.

Where liberals tend to blame America and Christianity, conservatives tend to reject out-of-hand any possibility that America's actions could in any way – no matter how remote or indirect – contribute to radicalization and the growth of militant Islam. It is the latter point of view that is by far the most dangerous, because it prevents us from understanding the motivations of our enemy and thereby impedes us in our efforts to defeat them, where blaming ourselves does not inherently prevent us from seeing the correct solution. It is also incredibly arrogant to *refuse to believe* that the righteous actions of your country could in any way contribute to radicalization, due to the fact that they are righteous. I am speaking to you, Dana Perino, and those who share your view on this subject.

Americans are not immune to cultural neuroses, and we have a few of our own. The most egregious and public example I have seen as relates to radicalization came from Fox News' Dana Perino on *the Five*. Perino said she would *never* believe that American actions have anything to do with radicalization. What an extremely arrogant and stupidly closed-minded attitude! I generally like and respect Perino a lot and have long thought of her as a highly intelligent person, but this attitude is simply moronic. The problem is that it is shared by a great many on the conservative side, and a lot of people take a lot of stock in Perino's opinions. It is a problem because vehemently refusing to believe that American actions could in any way contribute to radicalization and the rise of militant Islam blinds us to the motivations and mentality of the enemy, making it exponentially more difficult if not impossible to defeat them. Let's just willingly blind ourselves to the possibilities we do not find palatable and which do not fit with our world view, shall we? Perino is not an idiot by any stretch of the imagination. Why she holds such an idiotic position on the issue of radicalization is beyond me. I guess she is, at least in part, a product of our own uniquely American cultural neurosis.

So, let's shake off that cultural neuroses and take a look at how our actions play to the cultural neuroses of the Arab-Islamic world, thereby fueling the greatest rise in militant Islam this world has ever seen. Let's consider for a little while the completely fucked up world view that is prevalent and gaining influence in the Arab-Islamic world. Let's consider how this neurotic world view drives radicalization, and let's consider how our own institutionalized idiocy causes us to act in ways that feed directly into these epidemic neuroses and thereby create many more Islamic militants than we kill.

THE CRUSADES REDUX

I have written a good bit in this book on the fact that we only know one way to fight a war, and that way is conventional. I have said that our conventional war fighting feeds into the cultural neuroses that drive radicalization. Now it's time to explain in a little bit greater detail. Once you understand how what we do feeds into these neuroses, you will understand why we must use another strategy.

What is the first instinct of the great powers of America and the modern West when it comes to fighting a war? Bomb the hell out of them! Bombing the hell out of them has been proven to be an effective if not essential component of modern conventional warfare. It works quite well against conventional armies and nations. It works considerably less well against an unconventional enemy, and it works not at all and is in fact counterproductive when it comes to an unconventional enemy possessed of and driven by a radical militant religious ideology and a persecution complex stemming from the Crusades.

Of course, we might figure this out if we were weren't purposefully and even gleefully in denial of the Islamic nature of our enemy. Maalouf notes that they feel the Crusades very deeply, even today, as an act of rape. Think about that for a moment. These people truly although quite neurotically feel the pain of the Crusades even through the intervening centuries. Time is not a filter for them, and it does not heal their wounds. They feel quite incorrectly like they are constantly under attack from the West. It's a persecution complex, and our strategy and tactics play right into it.

How do you think they feel when we use the incomparable might of our air power to turn one of their cities to rubble? Of course we think they should understand that we are fighting a defensive war and are just doing what is necessary to win from the air. **They don't think like that**. All they see is a modern Western power flattening their city – their homes and businesses and infrastructure – and turning their world upside down. They see it as a continuation of the Crusades – as a continuing act of rape. Maalouf put it as well as it could possibly be put.

It is this persecution complex which drives radicalization and recruiting in response to our actions, no matter how justified and how measured we may believe they are. That's why pictures of bombed out cities are such an effective recruiting tool. They make a great rallying cry for those afflicted with this cultural neurosis. Since it seems the only way we know to "liberate" a city these days is to level it, we enable them in their neurosis. We reinforce their cultural persecution complex. We bolster their recruiting. We ratchet up the intensity of their hatred and their desire for what they feel to be legitimate revenge.

It's not *just* the fact that we level their cities that feeds into their persecution complex. It's also who we are. We are America and the infidel West. We're the ones they feel are always persecuting them. We're their natural enemy. It's also the way in which we level their cities. We do it with such an extreme advantage that they see it to be wholly unjust, unfair, and evil. They have no real, meaningful defense against our air power. They may luck out and shoot down a plane every now and then, but they have no effective means of defending their homes and their cities and their livelihoods from our overwhelmingly superior air power. That makes our use of air power in this way all the more egregious in their eyes. Can you see how this only plays into their persecution complex? Can you see how we may indeed kill a bunch of them and destroy their infrastructure this way but in the process fan the flames of their neurosis and bolster their recruiting? Can you see how we are only making the radicals more radical and creating far more new radicals than we kill? It's pretty easy.

Then there's the way we fight ground wars. We like to do it with large occupying armies. Of course, we only seem to know or have the stomach for conventional warfare, and when we are in a conventional war against a conventional enemy, this is the way to do it. It's not the way to do it when you're fighting an unconventional enemy driven by a persecution complex and a twisted, radical religious ideology of jihad. All they see is a Western army in their land – an infidel western army making mischief in their land. This is just another way to continue the Crusades. This is just another act of rape. Add in the fact that the only way we have of effectively clearing cities is to kick in doors and thereby terrorize the indigenous population and turn their lives upside down, and the rape is that much worse. Then, just like the bombing, there is the issue of overwhelming force. Nobody likes to feel as if they never have a fighting chance, and this feeling only intensifies their neurosis and their desire for revenge.

It was the presence of the American military as an occupying army in Iraq and the tactics we employed and the unfortunate abuses perpetrated by a few that gave rise to the Islamic State. Al Qaeda was in Iraq in insignificant numbers prior to the Iraq war. It was our bombing, our presence there as an occupying army, and our tactics that fostered the growth of Al Qaeda in Iraq, which would later morph into what is now the Islamic State. Everything we did played directly into the cultural neurosis – the cultural persecution complex – that radicalizes and grows this particular enemy.

I know there are a lot of uberconservatives out there

who are dismissing this as hogwash because it doesn't fit the conservative world view held by a great many that there is no way our actions have any effect on radicalization. If you are one, then I encourage you to disabuse yourself at once of that childish and simplistic world view and join reality. Although we don't do it intentionally, we create far more radicals than we kill with these boneheaded conventional strategies and tactics. My men and I have interviewed hundreds of Arab Muslims, and to the last one they all feel that the actions of the Islamic State and other militant Islamic groups – even those from across the Shia-Sunni schism – are a direct reaction to the actions of the Christian West and are at least partially if not wholly justified. They all pointed to the actions of the modern Western powers as the most direct driver of radicalization, though they don't see it as radicalization *per se*. We have no hope of prevailing against this enemy unless we realize that it is our strategy and tactics that have played into their cultural neurosis and radicalized them and then change our strategy and tactics accordingly.

Of course, in the development of our strategy and tactics, there is another cultural neurosis which must be taken into account, and it comes straight from the enemy's religious ideology. It is the firmly held but neurotic belief that they are entitled to all Arab lands and indeed to spread their brand of Islam to the entire world by force. Fair-minded people can see the Crusades for what they were – a Christian reaction to what they justifiably felt was a Muslim invasion of Jewish and Christian lands. Indeed, Muslims are the Johnny-come-lately of religion compared to Judaism and Christianity. Everywhere Muslims are, there was someone else there first, and they were most likely Jewish or Christian. The Crusades are probably most fairly seen as a push back against the Muslim taking of Jewish and Christian lands, including, quite importantly, the Holy Land. Even fair-minded Muslims understand this. The problem is we are not dealing with fair-minded Muslims.

These militant Islamic groups truly believe that they have been given their lands by Allah and have even been directed by him to bring the whole world into their version of Islam. They believe their god has destined them to bring the whole world under his rule. This cultural neurosis manifests itself in both an extreme fanaticism and an extreme sense of entitlement to do whatever is necessary to win the jihad and bring the whole world into the service of Allah according to their brand of Islam. They don't think they have ever *taken* anything from anyone. They merely accept what Allah has seen fit to give them, even if they have to take it from someone else by force.

How do you defeat an enemy whose parent culture is so neurotic? How do you vanquish an enemy which derives a net benefit – and a considerable one at that – from everything you know how to do to fight a war? If you're the United States, you don't. That's because we are incapable as a country and as a culture of ridding ourselves of the cancer of geopolitical and geosocial correctness. The same can be said for the rest of the modern West. We are so far gone into our institutionalized idiocy that we are unable to do anything meaningful to stop the rise of militant Islam or effectively defend ourselves and our interests against it. That is the sad but honest truth. We are doomed, but we don't *have* to be. We can find away around the institutionalized idiocy and the inertia. We just have to start thinking unconventionally.

First and most importantly you change your strategy and tactics so that everything you do doesn't play into the cultural neurosis of the population from which the enemy draws support. You develop a strategy that avoids to the greatest extent possible doing anything that plays into the cultural neuroses of your enemy's parent culture. To be able to formulate this strategy, you not only have to understand the cultural neuroses at work, but you also have to understand why we are losing the War on Terror and you have to understand the situation on the ground in the Islamic State theater of operation.

4
Abject Failure: The War on Terror

This, one of the shortest chapters in this book, is the one which is sure to draw the most criticism. Of course, I have already opened myself to attack by stating point-blank that the War on Terror has been and continues to be an abject failure. I am not backing off of that. Have we done some good? Sure we have. Have our men and women in the military performed admirably? It is beyond question that they have. They are heroes one and all, and I will honor them and sing their praises 'til the cows come home. My problem is with the *institution* of the military and the civilian command structure all the way up to the White House. My problem is with the institution that is incapable of developing an unconventional strategy and tactics which compliment it. My problem is with the total politicization of the war fighting process from soup to nuts. War may be nothing more than politics by other means, but you have to take the politics out of war fighting. My problem is with the fact that, despite the bravery and the sacrifices of our men and women who so gallantly fill those boots on the ground, militant Islam is 20 times what it was on 9/11. In any war, having an enemy far greater in number, range, influence, and resources after over 13 years of war than it was at the beginning can only be defined as abject failure.

The way things are now, we are going to have to stay in Afghanistan forever or it will become even more of a hotbed of militant Islam than it has ever been. That may happen even if we stay, if we continue to ignore the Islamic nature of the enemy and continue to adhere to the strategy and tactics that have been so successful **at growing the enemy** over the last 13+ years. The Islamic State is growing its numbers, its territory, and its sphere of influence in the Middle-East despite our involvement. Militant Islam is spreading its carcinogenic tentacles in Africa, Asia, and the Pacific. They are in Europe, and they are here. They are recruiting more and more Westerners and gaining more and more support. They clearly have a winning strategy, and we are utterly and embarrassingly unable to adapt our own strategy to meet it. We just keep stupidly doing the same thing over and over again, knowing it is not working but hoping against hope that, if we just stick to it, it will magically begin to work.

Our lack of imagination and creativity and adaptability is shocking and shameful, but not nearly as shocking and shameful as our sad state of intractable denial and our gleeful departure from reality in the name of geopolitical and geosocial correctness. These are some of the ugliest aspects of our institutionalized idiocy, and they are what has been losing the War on Terror for us for well over a decade and will secure the ultimate victory for the enemy – militant Islam. This is not hyperbole. This is not exaggeration. It is simply the honest truth we all need to wake up and see.

The problem is partially due to our outstanding performance and stunning success in the Gulf War. We felt like we had shaken the lingering specter of the quagmire that was Vietnam. We had the greatest military in the world, and nobody was going to whip us. We rode high on that victory for a decade, as well we should have. We defeated the fifth-largest army in the world in short order. It was a victory for the free world. It made us feel like we could handle any foe.

That was a conventional war, though, fought against a conventional enemy. In the conventional warfare arena, America and the modern West have unquestionable supremacy. In the unconventional warfare arena, fighting a war against an enemy driven by religious fanaticism and cultural neuroses, **we suck**. We suck because, in our arrogance, we think any enemy who makes war on us has to prosecute that war on our terms, and we are incapable of recognizing when they are not. Does anybody remember how well that worked for us in Vietnam? I believe we got our conventional forces bogged down in a war against an unconventional enemy and lost. We suck because we are overly concerned – preoccupied, even - with what the rest of the world thinks about us. We are so caught up in this phony enlightenment that we truly believe that we can enhance our national security by making the whole world love us. We think the way to do that is to be as agreeable as possible. We try to show the world that we are not a colonial power, so we shrink our sphere of influence. That hurts not only us but the ones we hang out to dry in the process. We have to show how enlightened and tolerant we are, so we **adamantly refuse** to acknowledge the Islamic nature of our enemy like a two-year-old refusing to take a nap or eat her vegetables. I guess it is more important to us that we not be seen as being at war with Islam than that we actually continue on as a free country. By all means, let's sacrifice ourselves and our country and our posterity on the altar of geopolitical and geosocial correctness.

In Afghanistan, which is where the War on Terror has been fought, primarily, we had a good deal of success against the Taliban. We basically decimated them. We have not been able to legitimately claim the same type of success against Al Qaeda. Why? Because the Taliban is conventional, and Al Qaeda is unconventional. We are great against conventional enemies. Of course, we could have been even greater, and we could have been out of Afghanistan in a relative blink of an eye if we weren't so fucking afraid of what the rest of the world thinks of us – if we were more concerned with our own national security and longevity as a free country.

Afghanistan is still a breeding ground for militant Islam. Even though we are still there in not insignificant numbers, it is a breeding ground for hatred of the infidel West. If we weren't there at all, it would look like Iraq and Syria before long. The Islamic State is already there, and their numbers there are growing rapidly. None of this would likely be the case if we had insisted on a secular government *as we damn well should have* instead of being so concerned about the way we look to the rest of the world.

The Iraq war is often conflated with the War on Terror, and understandably so, since it was, after the initial military victory, more of a counterinsurgency war against Islamic militants. I wouldn't object to the notion that the Iraq war *became* a theater of the War on Terror, but it didn't start out that way. It started out as a war to enforce U.N. resolutions that Saddam Hussein did not want to comply with. Our best intelligence, which turned out to be faulty, was that Saddam Hussein was actively re-developing Iraq's nuclear, biological, and chemical warfare programs. Saddam's defiant behavior and the faulty intelligence drew us and our allies into that entirely just war. (Iraq was in violation of U.N. Resolutions and their inspection requirements.) Our presence there as an occupying army, however, drew Al Qaeda and other militant Islamic groups. Now much of Iraq is in the hands of the Islamic State.

Militant Islam is gaining popularity and legitimacy not only in the Arab-Islamic world but in the world as a whole. Their online recruiting is phenomenal, and their messaging is exactly what it needs to be. They are even recruiting heavily from within the United States and other countries of the modern West. There are more militant Islamic groups that have been formed after 9/11 than existed before. We are losing the War on Terror in grand fashion. Militant Islam is inexorably on the rise. Militant Islam is inexorably on the march to our own back yards.

I know a lot of people are going to point to the current strength and resources of Al Qaeda and use that to say we are not losing the war and that the war has not been an abject failure. Al Qaeda may be down significantly from its peak, but it was a small, rag-tag group at 9/11, and it is now a small, rag-tag group. How is that success? 13+ years, and we have failed to eradicate them. The greatest military on Earth has had over 13 years to eradicate a small, rag-tag group of terrorists, and we have utterly failed. We have failed because, for some totally fucked up reason, we can't get our heads around the fact that we must fight an unconventional campaign which capitalizes on the Islamic nature of the enemy.

Furthermore, I know I am going to get a lot of comments to the effect of, "look what we've done to Al Qaeda." **The waning of Al Qaeda is not attributable to us.** We have really not put a dent in them. Their waning is attributable directly to the rise of the Islamic State. Have we taken out high value target after high value target with our drone strikes? Yes. Have we captured some of their leaders? Yes. Have other leaders come along to fill these voids? Of course, they have. Decapitation strikes only work against conventional enemies, though. They are not effective against enemies like Al Qaeda and the Islamic State. They can in fact be counterproductive, because they turn the killed leaders into martyrs and serve as recruiting tools and rallying cries. The truth is there isn't a damn thing we have done to Al Qaeda that has set them back for more than a few days.

Al Qaeda is waning because the Islamic State is waxing, and waxing big time. Not only does the Islamic State have vastly more resources than Al Qaeda, but they are masters of messaging. They are Internet savvy, and they know just how to market their brand. They are hip, and they know just how to glorify and romanticize their jihad so as to appeal not only to the Arab-Islamic world but to many in the rest of the world – even the modern West. The Islamic State and its associated groups are sucking up all the media attention and the resources and the recruits from the somewhat less barbaric Al Qaeda. Perhaps it is the very barbarism of the Islamic State that forms the basis of its appeal to so many. Again, no, we don't get credit for the wane of Al Qaeda. The Islamic State does. Do you think they are in Afghanistan to join forces with Al Qaeda and the Taliban? No, they are there to take over the show.

Oh, and don't go bringing up the fact that we got Bin Laden as evidence that we are winning the War on Terror. That is utter nonsense. It was a symbolic victory at best and did little if anything to change the landscape of the war. The people back home needed Bin Laden to die, but his death did not change a damn thing. Al Qaeda didn't all just up and lay down their AKs when we got the bastard. We are not winning the War on Terror, and nobody with any sense thinks we are.

The War on Terror is an abject failure and will continue to be so because of our boneheadedness. **It has been over 13 years and we still haven't figured this out!** How stupid can we be? When we see that our only successes have come against the conventional enemy – the Taliban - and that militant Islam continues to grow at a historic pace despite the blood and treasure we keep pouring into this war, we shouldn't take 13 years to figure out that we need to do something different. We need an entirely new strategy, and we need new tactics that fit it.

Our presence in Afghanistan and Iraq as an occupying army kicking in doors and our use of overwhelming air power to liberate cities by leveling them have done more to grow militant Islam than anything. Our strategy and our tactics have done exponentially more to strengthen our enemy and legitimize its cause not only in the Arab-Islamic world but the world as a whole than droning, Abu Ghraib, and Guantanamo combined. We seem bound and determined to stick with the same strategy no matter what. Why? Because we are absolute fucking idiots; that's why.

Again, we must change our strategy and tactics. We are doomed if we don't. That much should be abundantly clear. We should consider a name change for this war, because it's not terror we are fighting but militant Islam. Since this is what our enemy calls it, I suggest we simply call it the jihad. Regardless of what we call it, though, the strategy must take into full account the Islamic nature of our enemy as well as the situation on the ground.

5
Quagmire: The Situation on the Ground

$3BILLION FOR WHAT?

Since August of 2014, we have spent $3Billion just on the war against the Islamic State in Syria and Iraq. We continue spending $9Million every day. What is this all getting us? Precious little. We are training a whopping 60 Syrians to fight IS. We are training a few hundred and *maybe* up to a few thousand Iraqis to fight IS. The Kurds have a tentative hold on Kobani but are subject to a new IS offensive in the area and aren't getting any direct support from us. The Iraqis (really the Shia militias and some Iranian Quds) reportedly have an extremely precarious hold on Tikrit, and they have only been able to manage this with the aid of our new prom date who we dumped our original prom date for – Iran – and the Shia militias. In the meantime, IS has strengthened its hold on Mosul and placed more mines and booby traps, they have expanded their territory to include 50% of the land area in Syria and 60% of Anbar Province in Iraq. They have captured the extremely important Iraqi city of Ramadi with barely the semblance of a fight from the Iraqis, giving them access to even more oilfields and pipelines. They have strengthened their hold on Fallujah, and they are steadily enlarging their support zone. They're actually poised for a major offensive on Baghdad. $3Billion, and we haven't even really been able to trip them up or slow them down in any meaningful way. They are in Lebanon and Egypt and Libya, and they are operating in Kuwait. They are helping to grow Boko Haram in Nigeria and elsewhere in Africa. Despite the $3Billion spent, the Islamic State is growing at an astounding pace. What a waste!

We are crippled by a lot of factors that are part and parcel to our institutionalized idiocy. We are trying to fight it as a conventional war. We are trying to improve our image in the Arab-Islamic world and the world as a whole, so we hold back and expect the Arabs to take the lead and do the brunt of the work. We politicize everything about this war, right down to target selection and the rules of engagement. We have no HUMINT, so we are having a hell of a time finding things to bomb, anyway. 73% of sorties flown return with no weapons fired. **73% come back with all their munitions.** This is absolutely insane. Pilots report that they are hamstrung by the moronically political rules of engagement and target selection and approval. What are we doing up there?

To top it all off, many of the targets we do strike are bad targets altogether. Some are facilities IS used to use but no longer do. Others are places IS was holed up weeks prior but which have been deserted. Still others are facilities IS never has come near. I know this because my advance teams have seen bombing raids conducted on such places. No IS anywhere near, none around for weeks, if ever, then all of a sudden ... boom! The place is leveled. I understand we have to look like we're doing something, but come on! This is a giant waste of taxpayer money, and all this kind of destruction does is inflame the passions of the people from whom IS draws most of their support and recruits. Genius! Let's have some more of that!

We have sent 450 more advisors to Iraq. I wonder who they're advising. This is on top of the $25Billion we've already wasted training the Iraqi Army since the Iraq War. Wasn't the Iraqi Army trained already? I wonder what we're training them to do ... run away and leave U.S. material for the Islamic State to have? Well, they have been doing a damn fine job of that!

We're now getting Iran involved, too. Some of my sources tell me that we not only turned a blind eye to Iranian Quds force involvement in Iraq in the battle to retake Tikrit but that we requested or arranged it. Many think we are looking to Iran to stabilize Iraq. That's simply stupid. That's like hiring a convicted arsonist to house sit for you while you're on vacation. When it comes to militant Islam, the enemy of my enemy is not necessarily my friend. Just because there is this Shia-Sunni rift, we think we can exploit it and get the Shia on our side. This is the same Shia who chant "death to Israel" and "Death to America" in the streets of Tehran and Beirut and Gaza City. If there was a Nobel Prize for stupidity, America would definitely be in the running. So would the rest of the modern West.

We refuse to arm the Kurds directly. The geniuses in Washington think it best to work through the Iraqi government in Baghdad. Riiiiight! The Kurds are separatists. They are no friends of Baghdad, and Baghdad is no friend of theirs. They are not even Islamic, and this may be why they are the only ones doing anything meaningful against IS. They don't care what the world thinks of them as long as they survive.

What does this all add up to?

ONE LARGE ORDER OF QUAGMIRE FOR HERE, PLEASE!

This war (speaking only of the war against the Islamic State) is, in the estimation of most of the experts, a *generational* war. Even the most wildly, insanely optimistic predictions are that, with our current "strategy," we will defeat IS in three years. I am not sure what it is about the stunning ineffectiveness of the "strategy" after a year of application that would lead anyone with a brain to believe that it could result in the defeat of the Islamic State in three years or even three hundred. I am not sure what these people have been smoking, but I want some! IS has exploded over the last year. By that reasoning, I should loose 20 pounds in the next 10 years if I just keep doing what I did that caused me to gain 40 in the last two years. We are walking into this quagmire with a stupid grin on our face.

Vietnam looks like solid bedrock compared to this war. We have an extremely unconventional enemy which we are utterly unwilling or unable to recognize as such and adjust our strategy and tactics accordingly. We are so arrogant we think we can fight this war on *our* terms. We have an enemy that is driven by a fanatical and radical religious ideology and a culturally-ingrained persecution complex, and we adamantly refuse to acknowledge this. We refuse to even make a stab at understanding our enemy for fear of being seen as Islamophobic bigots by countries that have never given a shit about us and never will. We are showing that we are willing to make things even worse by exploiting the civil war between the Shia and Sunni. We are playing politics at every turn. Politics determines our rules of engagement and target selection and approval. Politics determines who we will train and supply directly and who we won't. We even have a schizophrenic approach to the whole damn situation. On the one hand, we want to pass this off as an Arab problem, but on the other, we want to be in charge and tell everybody how to fix it. Due to our suicidal preoccupation with geopolitical and geosocial correctness, **we have no clue what we are doing**, yet we are marching steadily into another, much worse Vietnam. Hell, the War on Terror has already lasted longer than Vietnam, and we have about as much to show for it. Fewer dead Americans, though, thank God.

This war is a quagmire, and everybody with a lick of sense knows it. Even the Defense Intelligence Agency Director sees it, and he's an institutional man! It's a quagmire of our own making, too. We cannot deny that it is our own actions and our own policies and our own strategy that make it such a quagmire. We are going to get bogged down in the politics and the geopolitical and geosocial correctness of it all. We are so worried about our reputation that we are willing to stretch a war which could be won in a year or less with the proper strategy (the war against IS) out into a *generational* war. We are going to get sucked in bit by bit just like we did in Vietnam. We are going to continue to refuse to acknowledge the nature of the war and the enemy, so we are going to continue to fight it as a conventional war, whether directly or by proxy. Therefore, everything we do will be counterproductive. Large Western or Western-funded armies will occupy Muslim Lands. Doors will be kicked in. Cities will be turned to rubble by the application of overwhelming air power. Not only will this be ineffective, but it will feed into the cultural neuroses which drive radicalization. Infrastructure will be destroyed. A few Islamic militants will be killed, but IS will only grow, because this will be seen in much of the Arab-Islamic world as a continuation of the Crusades. We will insert ourselves into the middle of the Sunni-Shia civil war. We will soon be neck-deep with no way out.

The war will inevitably come here, and we will continue fighting it the same way, because we are idiots. We are doomed.

6
The Strategy to Win: Making Our Own Destiny

GET SMART

I will say it again. We are doomed, but we don't have to be. We are bound to be subjugated by militant Islam and subjects under the tyranny of the harshest application of Sharia law, *but it doesn't have to be so.* We *can* snatch victory from the jaws of defeat, change our fate, and reclaim our rightful position as the masters of our own destiny. We are only doomed if we continue as we are under the iron reign of institutionalized idiocy and conventional "wisdom." The first and most essential thing we have to do to defeat and destroy militant, radical fundamentalist Islam and win the war on terror for good is to get smart. I have been witness to decades of the dumbing down of America, and I'm telling you we have to snap out of it before it's too late.

The institutionalized idiocy of political and social

correctness has us thinking it is somehow wrong or that we are somehow less than human and definitely not enlightened or civilized if we recognize the religious nature of the enemy. We live in an insane world where we are labeled Neanderthals if we fail to reject out of hand the idea that a religious ideology could be the driver of a war. We are deathly afraid of being seen as making war on Islam – so afraid in fact that we will adamantly refuse to recognize that it is indeed a popular and growing part of the religion of Islam that is making war on us. We are so afraid of being seen as making war on Islam that we will refuse to acknowledge the religious nature of this war even to our own defeat and subjugation. We have to get smart and stop ignoring and even flatly rejecting the painfully obvious truth that **jihad** is being waged on us. Like it or not, we are in a religious war – a holy war. Once we allow ourselves to realize and accept this fact, we can use it to our advantage in several ways.

First, once we acknowledge and accept the religious driver of the jihad, we can familiarize ourselves with the ideologies involved and their context in the world at large and the world of war in particular. Once we understand our enemy, as we absolutely must, we can figure out how to defeat them, destroy them, and forever discredit the ideologies that drive their jihad against us. Understanding the key aspects of the religious ideologies driving our enemy, we can turn what they believe to be their strengths into terminal weaknesses. The very things they believe are what make them so powerful that they are destined to rule the world can be taken advantage of by an enlightened and intelligent enemy (us), turned against them, and indeed be their very undoing.

Second, acknowledging that religious ideologies are the drivers of the jihad in which we are reluctantly engaged and understanding those ideologies together with their geosocial context allows us to formulate a strategy and develop tactics that will have the greatest deleterious effect on the enemy while **not** simultaneously having the unintended inverse effect of creating more of the enemy than we kill. I have shown earlier in this book how our willful ignorance of the religious ideologies of our enemy as drivers of their aggression against us has resulted our employing of a strategy and tactics that have *actually caused* unprecedented growth of our enemies number, power, influence, and perceived legitimacy in the Arab world and the world at large. Understanding our enemy and what motivates them will enable us to reverse this course and chart a new one which will lead to victory in the short term and the certainty that we will not have to face the same enemy again later in the long term.

Third, acceptance of the inescapable fact that this is a religious war waged against Christianity and the modern West by militant, radical fundamentalist Islam allows us to get our messaging right. It allows us to cast our cause most favorably and the enemy's cause most unfavorably on the geopolitical and geosocial landscapes. The more clearly and accurately the roles of aggressor and victim are defined, and the more clear it is made that we are in a war of right versus wrong – good versus evil – the more support we will find for our cause in this world.

Fourth, an informed acceptance of the religious nature of this war and the fact that our enemies are driven primarily by warped religious ideologies which seek to end not only our religion but our very way of life and to subjugate us to their twisted religious law will ensure we have the support we need at home to win this jihad quickly and never face a jihad from this enemy again. Religion is one of the all-time greatest motivators of war, and more men have been killed in the name of the advancement of a religious ideology or the freedom from the imposition of one than in the pursuance of any other cause. The people will get behind this war once they are shown the stark reality that *their* freedom of religion, and indeed *their* freedom from the imposition of the twisted religion that drives our enemy, is what's at stake.

Another part of getting smart is realizing what we can count on and what we can't. We can't count on Arabs to fight other Arabs with the 110% level of commitment that is needed to win this jihad ... except when it comes down to the Sunni-Shia split. Arabs have a very, very strong cultural -historical identity. It would be just as realistic as the prospect of getting Americans to go to war against other

Americans in this day and age. In order to get Arabs to fight other Arabs with the intensity and commitment levels that are necessary, we would have to exploit the rift between the Sunni and Shia sects of the Islamic faith. The wisdom of doing this on a grand geopolitical and georeligious scale is debatable given that both Shia and Sunni have their militant extremists. We will take up that debate later in this chapter. Absent the exploitation of that rift, which is not an inconsiderable one, it is simply a lame-brained idea to think that Arabs will go to war against other Arabs with the fight-to-the-end dedication that is necessary if we are going to eradicate militant Islam once and for all.

This is in no way an insult to the Arab people and culture. It is a testament to a great quality that we as Americans and the people of every other great culture and nationality share and indeed pride ourselves on. Cultural identity and cohesiveness is what allows great societies and cultures such as that of which we speak to flourish. Cultural and national loyalty – and to a great extent religious loyalty like that we see with Islam – are essential threads in the fabric of every great culture and every great nation this world has ever seen, and that is to be appreciated.

There is yet another aspect of getting smart, and that is understanding and accepting our place in this world. We must realize and come to terms with what the proper global role of the modern West in general and America in particular is. Unless we understand, accept, and exploit the hegemony of the modern West in general and the United States in particular, we cannot hope to effectively address regional problems which are in actuality nascent global threats and therefore pose a direct, clear and present danger to the liberty and safety of America and the free world.

Like it or not, the United States of America has been the hegemon since the end of WWII. Many great nations of the modern West have joined us as under-hegemons and have acted as a sort of world police for decades, whether independently, jointly or at the behest of the United Nations. What is really so bad about this? Think of the alternative. Our current President and many others of his ilk would like to undo this situation and establish a new world order of live and let live, or more accurately, live and let die. To every nation and every culture self determination no matter what the cost or the result. No American exceptionalism. No hegemony of the modern West with the United States at the helm. In this view, America and the modern West have acted not just as the world police but as dirty cops in this role, imposing their will by force on unwilling peoples. It is *we* who have been the evildoers. Just ask our President's long-time preacher Jeremiah Wright. We are getting what we deserve for our constant, unjustified, and imperialistic meddling. America's chickens are coming home to roost. Bullshit!

America and the modern West are not without their blemishes, but far, far, far more often than not, we have been a force for good and against evil in this world. Have there been instances where we projected force when we shouldn't have? Sure, but there have also been instances where we should have projected force but just sat on our hands, because we were afraid of what the rest of the world would think. In fact, the rest of the world was looking to America and the modern West for leadership. We have been the accepted hegemon for so long that many nations will not act without our approval and leadership – even in the case of genocide. The growing cancer of geopolitical and geosocial correctness has caused us to be uncomfortable in our hegemony for some time. We must find the comfort again! We must – even if reluctantly - accept the hegemony of America and the modern West and use that position for good. We are doomed if we don't.

It is the rejection of this hegemony and the failure to diagnose and treat the self-induced psychosis of geopolitical and geosocial correctness that has given rise to our current non-strategy strategy regarding the Islamic State in the micro and militant Islam in the macro.

THE REQUIREMENTS OF A SUCCESSFUL STRATEGY

Any strategy hoping to defeat and destroy the Islamic State and eradicate militant Islam must have all of the following characteristics:

First, it must erode the morale of the enemy combatants. Eroding their morale makes them less effective fighters. It also carries over to the supporting population. There is no way to hide low morale, and declining morale is contagious. It is hard to support fighters who are losing their fighting spirit. The further we erode their morale, the further we erode their support in the Arab-Islamic world and the world as a whole.

Second, it must frustrate recruiting and online radicalization. To be successful, a strategy must make it less and less attractive to be a part of IS and militant Islam in general. All we have been doing the last 14 years is making it more and more attractive to join up. We have quite stupidly failed to realize that our tactics and even our strategy as a whole play into the cultural neuroses which feed militant Islam. While trying to kill it, we have inadvertently grown it, and our self-important and self-centered world view has blinded us to this fact. Now, the best way by far to frustrate recruiting is to make the population from which recruits are drawn believe militant Islam is a lost cause. Nobody wants to join a lost cause.

Third, it must be unconventional as hell and very low-intensity compared to conventional warfare. It cannot employ large occupying armies kicking in doors or the destructive use of air power. These only feed into those cultural neuroses I have been talking about. A guerrilla campaign would not only avoid feeding into those cultural neuroses, but it would be far more efficient and effective, bullet for bullet and soldier for soldier, but it will be far more affordable. Guerrilla warfare is relatively cheap, and we don't have to pay to rebuild destroyed infrastructure after it is all over. My fear is that there will be serious attacks on American soil causing many American deaths and injuries and that the knee-jerk reaction of massive retaliation will plunge us into a decades-long religious war which we can never win with that conventional, reactionary way of thinking.

Fourth, it must undermine the legitimacy of the militant Islamic groups in particular and the ideology of militant Islam in general. Nothing does this better than a guerrilla campaign where the enemy is consistently losing fighter after fighter and engagement after engagement to small units of an American infidel force which, in total, numbers only a fraction of the enemy's fighting force. The legitimacy of the enemy and the militant Islamic ideology to which the enemy subscribes will lose all legitimacy and credibility in first the world at large and then the Arab-Islamic world from which it draws the bulk of its support. How can the enemy be seen as pursuing the true cause and will of Allah if he is allowing them to be defeated by a small number of infidels?

Fifth, the strategy must include a robust psychological warfare campaign. This includes not only a direct campaign designed to accomplish the essential tasks of eroding the enemy's morale and hindering their ability to operate and to predict our movements but a global campaign that will exploit our victories on the ground to undermine the legitimacy of the enemy and the enemy's ideology in the Arab-Islamic world and the world as a whole.

Sixth, and lastly, the strategy must extend to all of militant Islam. It is not enough to defeat Al Qaeda or the Islamic State. If you pick one or two groups as your enemy, and you think the war is over when you feel you have defeated them, **you will never be free from the war that will forever be waged on you by the adherents of the ideology**. **You must defeat the militant Islamic ideology as a whole**. You must eradicate jihadism completely – *both* Sunni *and* Shia. You begin with the Islamic State and end with Iran. You start with the marquis name and get your statement victory. Then you pick off group after group, further eroding the legitimacy and credibility of militant Islam as you go. Once you have undermined this legitimacy and credibility and sufficiently eroded popular support for the regime – and only then – the regime can be toppled and a stable, moderate regime take its place. It is much easier to fell an obelisk once you have chipped its base away to almost nothing. The successful strategy involves working with the opposition in Iran from the beginning.

Our current non-strategy strategy has none of these essential characteristics. It isn't even coherent, and it may not be designed to defeat this enemy at all. Let's take a look.

OUR CURRENT NON-STRATEGY STRATEGY

Even President Obama admits that the United States has no complete and coherent strategy to deal with the Islamic State. One reason we are unable to develop a strategy is we are not even sure what our objective is – if it's to destroy them, to merely defeat them, or to just manage them. With no strategy for IS, we certainly can't even come close to a strategy for militant Islam as a whole. Why don't we have a strategy? We don't and likely never will have a strategy because of our institutionalized idiocy. We think this is an Arab problem for Arabs to take the lead in solving. We are willing to "assist," but that is it, and only if we can be in charge. We are in an acute delusional state which is threatening to become chronic. The delusional state has been brought on by the wholesale self-injection of the highly euphoric but radically debilitating drugs of political and social correctness.

We have deluded ourselves into believing that the Islamic State is the extent of the problem. We have deluded ourselves into believing that what is clearly a nascent global threat is only a regional Arab problem. We have deluded ourselves into thinking that our proper role is just to help the Arabs solve it – after we tell them how. We have deluded ourselves into thinking that the Arabs have the will and the capacity for wholesale slaughter of fellow Arabs necessary to defeat IS in the short run and militant Islam in the long run. Does anybody remember how long Jordan's offensive lasted after their pilot was burned alive in a cage by the Islamic State?

We are waiting to see what the Arabs are prepared to do and then base our strategy on that. If IS and militant Islam were truly just a regional Arab problem, I might be more inclined to get on board with such a strategy. They are a global problem now, though, and their aim is clearly world domination of their version of Islam and Sharia law. Unspeakable terror and carnage are just part of the process. Still we wait. We wait on the Arabs – the very Arabs who failed to recognize the problem and snuff it out while it was still just an Arab regional problem – to take the lead and be the solution, subject to our direction and approval. While the Islamic State takes more and more territory and captures city after town and increases its wealth and power and spreads its tentacles into Europe, Asia, the Pacific, and even America, we wait. While militant Islamic groups gain power and increase their barbarism in Africa and Yemen, we wait. We wait for the Arabs to take the lead and be the solution - the solution we can safely direct or "assist" from the sidelines. This is institutionalized idiocy.

It was the Arabs who allowed and in many instances *actually fostered* the phenomenal rise of militant Islam, so their track record in this department is, let's say, somewhat less than stellar. The Islamic State has a high level of Arab support, as do other groups from across the Shia-Sunni rift. Why do we expect the Arab people to unite against IS? Institutionalized idiocy. A non-strategy strategy born of institutionalized idiocy can never succeed.

Our development of any meaningful, coherent, effective strategy at the government level is further hindered by President Obama's completely asinine if not wholly insane pursuance of a nuclear deal with Iran at any cost and regardless of the terms. We keep gleefully allowing Iran to move the goalposts while we bask in the sweet intoxication of Islamophobia-fobia. This president seems to have such a skewed world view and be so far gone into the dementia of geopolitical and geosocial correctness that he believes his legacy as a peacemaker with Islam requires a deal with Iran – any deal – even the atrociously bad and dangerous one that has been reached. Either that, or he is bent on the destruction of the United States at the hands of militant Islam. He is either guilty of LWI – leading while intoxicated by his own self-generated hubris, or he is simply evil. I haven't made up my mind. Either way, this is not a foreign policy that could possibly ever lead to an intelligent strategy for IS and militant Islam.

So, what is the strategy that will succeed? Must the solution be an Arab one? Must the Solution be a global one led by the Arabs? Whether the solution is an Arab one, a global one, or an American one, can we annihilate them through the application of overwhelming force? Should we, even? What, then, is the best strategy – the strategy which gives us the greatest possibility of lasting success? Several have been offered, including the Arab solution, the global solution, and the who-gives-a-damn overwhelming force solution. I'll explain in turn why each solution is unacceptable then offer the one strategy which is most likely to end the cancer of militant Islam without leaving a festering ulcer on the landscape of the Arab culture and the religion of Islam.

THE ARAB SOLUTION

To a great extent, the Obama administration argues that the solution must be an Arab one. The policy is somewhat schizophrenic, though, because we *are* bombing. Never mind the fact that our air campaign is crippled by politically-motivated restrictions, rules of engagement, and target selection and approval as well as by a total lack of HUMINT. The policy is also schizophrenic because, while we say that the solution must be an Arab one, we insist that military action must be multilateral, taken by some vague, mythical coalition the member roles of which are amorphous at best. Some of the many shortcomings of this policy are readily evident from its scatterbrained nature alone, but let's take a look at its critical flaw.

The critical flaw of the Arab solution is two-fold.

First, it willfully and gleefully ignores the obvious fact that neither militant Islam as a whole nor the Islamic State as its flagship organization is a purely regional, purely Arab problem. IS and other militant organizations of both Shia and Sunni varieties have expanded beyond Arab lands into Asia, Africa, Europe, the Pacific, and even the United States. How can the Arab nations be expected to solve a global problem which is nothing more than the expression of what started out as a regional Arab problem but was ignored and to a significant degree fostered by Arabs?

No thinking person with a cursory knowledge of Arab history and social dynamics would think for a second that the Arab nations could solve the problem of militant Islam. Set aside the fact that the Arab nations do not have the military might and training or the funding necessary to defeat the Islamic State, let alone militant Islam as a whole using the conventional strategy and tactics the whole world is married to. We have been hearing rumblings for months about the formation of a joint Arab force to combat the Islamic State and Iranian-backed Shia militants, but what has really been done? Nothing meaningful, really. Then there is the popularity of the militant groups in the Arab-Islamic world. IS and other militant Islamic groups, both Sunni and Shia, are extremely popular among the Arab people as explained a few chapters back. No Arab nation will ever have the popular support necessary to eradicate any militant Islamic Arab group, especially not one that subscribes to the same sectarian beliefs.

How can we expect one group to go to war with the commitment necessary to win against another group that shares the same core defining beliefs? This is nothing but a delusional pipe dream. Sunni will never eradicate other Sunni, and Shia will never eradicate other Shia. It is as simple as that. There is no inducement large enough. The only way to even begin to approach the problem from the "Arab solution" mindset is to exploit the rift between the Shia and Sunni sects. Nothing good can come of this. It is nothing short of exacerbating an already complicated civil war among Arab peoples and within one of the largest religions in the world. How is that wise? If the Arab culture and the religion of Islam survived it, the remnant would surely bear an unprecedented hatred of the West for being the arbiter of such conflagration of fratricide. We would make a more powerful and determined enemy than the one we now face, *and one with real legitimacy*. We have already started down this road by accepting and possibly encouraging the involvement of Iranian Quds forces (Shia) and the Iraqi Shia militias in the fight against IS in Iraq. Why? You guessed it. Institutionalized idiocy.

Let's just step off into theory for a second here and say that we were able to successfully pit Shia against Sunni and defeat the Islamic State, Boko Haram, and other Sunni militants. We have to first realize what that would entail. It would entail the eradication of the entire Sunni sect by the

Shia sect. Not only does it radically alter Islam, but it sets up a situation where Shia militants are seen as the legitimate soldiers of Allah, having defeated the Sunni. We would be eliminating one branch of our enemy by radically strengthening another branch of our enemy both in terms of military force and and perceived credibility and legitimacy. Thus, while the divide and conquer approach may seem at first blush to have its advantages, upon critical analysis, it will do more harm than good to our overall strategy of the eradication of militant Islam. We are better off discrediting and delegitimizing both branches of our enemy instead of building up one branch we know we will only have to defeat later and at much greater cost. It's paying a hundred dollars down the road to save a dollar now. It's simply stupid. Enough of that talk. To attempt such an Arab solution would scar the religion of Islam and the Arab culture forever. There is no Arab solution that pits Sunni against Shia, and there is no Arab solution in general.

If the Arab world had the military capability, let alone the will, to solve the problem of militant Islam, it would have been solved long ago when it was truly just a regional Arab problem. It isn't politically expedient for Arabs to solve this problem, though. It never has been, and that is why they did not solve it when they could have. Is it even truly an Arab problem to begin with? Are we right to expect Arab nations to slay a monster *we* created, although inadvertently, *by our own hand*?

THE GLOBAL SOLUTION

Part of the current schizophrenic U.S. Policy is that the solution to the Islamic State and militant Islam must be a global one, with the auspices of Arab leadership while we call the shots behind the scenes, of course. The idea of true Arab leadership of such a solution is a nonstarter for the reasons just discussed. Not that true Arab leadership is what we actually want. Because of our institutionalized idiocy born of the delusional euphoria of geopolitical and geosocial correctness, we reject the legitimacy of American exceptionalism and of the hegemony of America and the modern West. We still want to run things, though. We should be wracked with cognitive dissonance. Because we reject American exceptionalism and hegemony, we lack the will to act unilaterally in any meaningful way. We see it as somehow wrong to defend ourselves and the world when the world will not act. Our defense, therefore, against the enemy of the Islamic State and militant Islam, is dependent on some magic number of significantly non-Western countries being on board with us. We will never do anything truly meaningful about the problem unless and until we have the support – even if in name only - of the requisite number of non-Western counties. Whether we would ever actually do anything meaningful even then is debatable.

The fallacy of the global solution is that there will never be a truly global solution. We will never have more than a few true partners in this effort, and guess what ... they will all be countries of the modern West. It will be in reality a solution of America and the modern West with a bunch of names of inconsequential non-Western countries on the cover sheet for appearances. It will still be a war funded and executed almost entirely by America and the modern West. Sure, from time to time countries like Jordan and Saudi Arabia will get involved in spurts to meet their own political or sectarian ends. We have seen the spurt of increased Jordanian involvement after the brutal immolation of their downed pilot on the Internet. We are now witnessing the increased involvement of Saudi Arabia (Sunni) against the Shia militants in Yemen, but that, too will wane with popular and political will just as did American involvement in Vietnam and more recently in Iraq and Afghanistan.

A truly global solution is impossible. If we sincerely wanted a truly global solution, we would have gone to the U.N. I think we all know what a dismal failure that would have been. Russia and China would not exactly be chomping at the bit to support us, and that's just the start of the difficulties of fashioning a truly global solution from the start. Too many cooks in the kitchen. One wants borscht, another wants General Tso's chicken, and yet another just wants a big, fat, juicy quarter-pounder with cheese. It doesn't work. Never has and never will. A truly global solution is an unattainable fantasy, and we know it, so we settle for the *appearance* of a global solution which, due to institutionalized idiocy, is doomed to solve exactly nothing.

The Arab-Islamic world will be able to see through the veneer of globalism and behold the solution for what it really is – an American-led solution carried out by America and the rest of the modern West using basically the same strategy and tactics we have employed since 9/11. They will see this as nothing more than a continuation of the Crusades, and though we may indeed kill a lot of Islamic militants, we will also level a lot of cities and kick in a lot of doors and piss off the greater part of the Arab-Islamic world, thereby inadvertently bolstering the enemy's recruiting and further cementing its already-solid determination. In short, we will create more radicals than we kill. Is that really what we need to be doing at this point in the game?

THE OVERWHELMING FORCE SOLUTION

I hear a lot of calls for the United States to just miraculously snap out of its sweet slumber of geopolitical and geosocial correctness and act unilaterally in a **BIG** way. I have heard calls for the annihilation of all Islamic militants through the massive application of air power (the turn the place into a parking lot approach), the marching of hundreds of thousands of troops through Iraq and Syria (the kick in every door approach), a combination of both, and even the use of nuclear weapons. Though I applaud the ones making these calls for being able to see through the smokescreen of bullshit with which the problem of the Islamic State and militant Islam is cloaked, they still have not seen far enough. None of the suggestions are acceptable, and I will explain why.

I have already shown in this book how the massive application of air power and the employment of large, occupying armies kicking in doors are actually counterproductive, as they are seen in Arab-Islamic culture as a rape of Muslim lands – a continuation of the Crusades – and will ultimately result in the creation of more radical Islamic militants who want to kill us than we kill in the process. The counter I hear back from the supporters of maximum force is that, if we simply go big enough and don't stop until the job is done, we will be able to kill every last one of them. Just like we did in Vietnam, huh? There is simply no way to kill off every one of the enemy this way, even if we deploy 100% of our air power and a million ground troops. We are not fighting a conventional state, and the enemy does not act like a conventional state. Many will run and hide in other countries where our application of such massive force will serve them well as a recruiting tool. Then it's a never-ending game of whack-a-mole. The massive application of force by a modern Western power against any Arab-Islamic group would be seen in that culture and likely in the rest of the world at large as unnecessarily barbaric and abusive action *based on religion*. This view would only be bolstered if we chased them through country after country leaving a path of destruction as we went. We would never be able to put a positive spin on it — even if it could work, which it can't.

Even assuming the outlandishly unrealistic possibility that we *could* kill every last Islamic militant with such a campaign and thus eradicate this cancer from the planet, we would never be able to do so without supermassive collateral damage. We would likely kill more noncombatants than combatants. We have already seen how we "liberate" cities ... by flattening them. To win through the application of overwhelming force would necessarily mean to lay waste to the entire region and to destroy the lives and livelihoods of millions of noncombatants. Lather, rinse, and repeat in every place the mole pops up next. Do we really want to invade, occupy, and destroy the infrastructure and economy of every place these douchebags pop up in this perverted game of whack-a-mole? Yeah, that would make us really popular. I can guarantee you it would win us more enemies than friends. Oh, and one more thing: who pays to rebuild?

Even if I was wrong on all of that, which I'm not, and even if it was the best way to win this jihad, how smart would it be to focus all of our military might on a relatively few militants when a resurgent Russia and a rising China are presenting evolving threats which may soon require the focus of our military might? Russia and China would be emboldened by the sight of the United States tying up all of its military and economic resources in the Middle East and wherever else militant Islam crops up. They would love that, and don't think for a second they would not take advantage of it. It is better to have our military available as a deterrent against aggression by these two countries than committed in a futile effort to eradicate militant Islam through the application of overwhelming conventional force. Overwhelming force works against conventional states with conventional armies – not against such an unconventional, asymmetric enemy as militant Islam. We got a taste of that in Vietnam, and an enemy driven by fanatical religious beliefs is an even more formidable foe.

I have heard some say that we could apply overwhelming force using just a few tens of thousands of ground troops and a robust air campaign. They say we could have them (the Islamic State) wiped out in a few months. We have been trying that for almost 14 years in Afghanistan, and it hasn't worked well for us. We have inadvertently created more radicals than we have killed using this approach. You still have the fatal flaws of the leveling of cities and the use of occupying, door kicking armies – flaws which play right into the cultural neuroses that radicalize otherwise moderate people. Massive air power and occupying armies of any size will be counterproductive. *We simply must stop playing into the cultural neuroses that create more Islamic militants.*

So, if the Arab solution is a hopeless pipe dream, the global solution is a fantasy, the current approach of limited war is not working, and the application of overwhelming force is a nonstarter, what else is there? There's the smart way. The way you eradicate a highly unconventional enemy driven by an extreme radical religious ideology is to think unconventionally yourself. We truly have very, very little unconventional and creative thought in this world when it comes to the problem of the Islamic State and militant Islam. *Every* anti-IS strategy offered publicly *from whatever source* has had one thing in common. **They are all conventional!** Nobody ... I repeat, nobody ... is thinking outside the box. It is a damn shame.

In the face of the unfamiliar – and especially in the face of such extreme terror as we see from IS, it is natural for most people to retreat to the comfortable – the conventional. We seek the comfort of the tried and true, but we fail to realize that what is tried and true under one set of circumstances may result in dismal failure under a different set of circumstances. It's great to fall back on the tired and true with conventional states like Russia and China, but with IS and militant Islam, it is utter folly. It is time to not just think outside the box but to set the damn box on fire and lay rubber as we speed pedal to the metal as far away from it as possible.

So far, *nobody* has advanced a strategy that will work – that isn't fatally flawed and obviously so when critically analyzed. Nobody *except Team Swandog*, that is. Team Swandog's unconventional, creative, and adaptive strategy is the only one being advanced that avoids playing into the cultural neuroses that create radicals in the first place. It is the only one that eradicates the enemy through the application of force in the microcosm but more importantly by delegitimizing the enemy and their core philosophy in the macro. No other strategy has a hope of permanently eradicating the enemy. Team Swandog's strategy *will* accomplish this by undermining the legitimacy of all militant Islamic ideologies (Sunni and Shia) in the eyes of the Arab-Islamic world and the world at large. Once the legitimacy of the ideologies is thoroughly undermined, they will disappear for good as has every other deligitimized ideology in history. Once a thing is completely discredited not just in the eyes of the intelligentsia but in the eyes of the world at large, it is relegated forever to the pages of history, and though there may be the occasional fanatic attempt at resurgence, it will never gain significant traction again. Here's how it's done.

THE TEAM SWANDOG SOLUTION

There is a way to rapidly and permanently rid the world of the evil ideology of militant Islam and all of its practitioners, both Shia and Sunni. There is a strategy to do so with minimal collateral damage, minimal noncombatant casualties, minimal friendly casualties, and minimal expense – in fact, the Islamic state could be eradicated for less than the $25Billion we have already *wasted* on the "training" of the Iraqi Army. The strategy I am referring to is private sector, unconventional & low intensity, and capitalizes on the nature of the enemy and the jihad, turning what the enemy (and to a great extent the rest of the world) perceives as its strengths into weaknesses that will be its quick and conspicuous undoing.

Private Sector

The Team Swandog solution isn't a government solution. Let's get that straight right off the bat. Expecting the government to get its head out of its ass is just sheer stupidity. Governments have this quality of being at once both the most irresistible force and the most immovable object in the world. Institutionalized idiocy is not easy if even possible to break a government of. No, this is a private sector solution. The governments of the world have bungled us into this situation. Do you really expect them to be able to just put their thinking caps on and get us out of it? They're too far gone into the self-delusion of supreme wisdom. No one can open their eyes and shake them back to reality, least of all me. Believe me; if I thought I could, I would have long ago testified to Congress and shown them the merits of an enlightened strategy. And what about the gridlock? Who could bust it to get anything through? Certainly not me! No one can suddenly and miraculously cure the party faction that serves as a constant preventative of meaningful action regarding the Islamic State and militant Islam. Of party faction, James Madison wrote in *The Federalist No. 10*:

> It is in vain to say that enlightened statesmen will be able to adjust these clashing interests, and render them all subservient to the public good. Enlightened statesmen will not always be at the helm. Nor, in many cases, can such an adjustment be made at all without taking into view indirect and remote considerations, which will rarely prevail over the immediate interest which one party may find in disregarding the rights of another or the good of the whole.

It's not just party faction that gets in the way. Divisions within parties are just as effective at preventing meaningful action. The same party controls both the House and the Senate, and still nothing worth a damn gets done. The President can't even get his own party solidly behind him on Trade! Does anybody seriously believe that this Congress, or any subsequent Congress for that matter, could somehow set aside all the competing allegiances and interests and do what is best for the country as a whole on such an incredibly divisive issue as the Islamic State and militant Islam? Dream on!

If the problem is going to be solved, it's going to be solved by the private sector – by people like you and me. The private sector is not nearly as firmly held in the vise of institutionalized idiocy as the government is. The private sector is more capable of thinking unconventionally and creatively than is the government or the military. Just look at the conventional thinking being offered up from those sectors (including retired military men who are now TV talking heads) as to how to handle the Islamic State. *Everybody* is thinking conventionally.

There is another advantage a private sector solution offers over a conventional state solution. The state solution would play into the cultural neuroses which drive radicalization. It would be viewed in a not insignificant part of the Arab-Islamic world (and the rest of the non-Western world as well) as a Western infidel power imposing by violent force its will and values and morality on innocent Arab Muslims. The private sector solution is one of people and not of state power. It will much more readily be seen as a defensive action – an action to preserve our freedom, our way of life, and even our right to live – instead of the imperialistic and unjust aggression that any state action by a Western power is so easily viewed as in the Arab-Islamic world and the larger non-Western world.

Private sector action holds yet another distinct and very desirable advantage over state action. There is a total lack of absurd, politically motivated, socially and politically correct rules of engagement. A civilian force could devote itself wholly to winning the war without such asinine considerations entering the picture. A civilian force doesn't have to worry about a legacy or an election. A civilian force would not be beholden to or answerable to any politician and would not be under the control of any president. It would be free to formulate the rules of engagement most advantageous to the aim of winning the war and eradicating the enemy.

Under the laws of war, such a force would be considered a militia. As a militia, its members would be entitled to the protections of the Geneva Conventions, not that the Islamic State or any other militant Islamic group would abide by the laws of war. Speaking of the laws of war, you may find it interesting that there is no international or federal law prohibiting citizens from engaging in combat against an enemy with which the United States is at war. We have heard of individuals and small groups planning to go engage with the Islamic State, and in some cases doing so, without so much as a suggestion that such would be violative of any federal or international law. That's because it clearly is not.

Now, there is what at first seems like a major and possibly fatal drawback to private sector, civilian action. Where state action comes with a mighty military machine and a seemingly infinite purse, private sector action appears to have no purse and cannot avail itself of the might of the military state. To the average, conventional thinker, this consideration alone is enough to discredit the entire idea of civilian militia action. Remember, though, what I have been saying about thinking creatively and unconventionally.

The unconventional and creative thinker can see an advantage here. Let's not kid ourselves, war is an expensive business, but guerrilla war is almost immeasurably cheaper than conventional state action. It's still not going to be a cakewalk to raise the needed cash, though. Difficulty, however, is no reason not to try. Difficult, yes; impossible, hell, no! The difficulty in funding and the smallness of the budget forces the tacticians of such a force to think more creatively and unconventionally, and the result is that they will get far more bang out of every buck than the mighty military machine so accustomed to the deep pockets of D.C. would. Also, the might of a state military machine is actually an impediment in a conflict such as this one. The possession of such might traps you into thinking within the context of its use. You develop tactics for the use of the assets you have, especially when they are by conventional wisdom far superior to anything else. You lose the ability to consider that which doesn't make full use of your might, as you see it. Applying this kind of thought in the conflict at hand is like trying to eat cake with a shovel or paint the Mona Lisa with a paint sprayer. The shovel may be bigger than the fork, and the paint sprayer may be more advanced than the brush, but they are simply not the right tools for the job. So the drawbacks of private sector civilian action are, when viewed with an open mind in the light of critical analysis and in the context of the conflict in which we are engaged, actually more advantage than disadvantage.

Unconventional & Low-Intensity ... but Fucking Relentless

We have already seen how conventional warfare is not

going to work. Conventional warfare will only scatter and grow the ideology. The delegitimizing and discrediting of the ideology and its practitioners is absolutely essential for victory, and a conventional military action does nothing of the sort. It may in *our* minds, but not in the minds of the Arab-Islamic world and not likely in the minds of the larger non-Western world. In reality, there would always be significant numbers of the enemy who would survive the onslaught. It simply isn't possible to kill them all through a conventional campaign, just like it isn't possible to eradicate a cockroach infestation by stomping on the roaches. Just like the roaches will scatter and scurry and go hide in the dark, so will the warriors of militant Islam when they see the boot of the American military bearing down on them. Those escaping the onslaught would be viewed by themselves and the Arab-Islamic world – and to a great extent by the entire non-Western world – as heroes who were allowed to survive by Allah's will and blessing. This would only empower them and aid their recruiting and fundraising. Rather than discrediting and delegitimizing the enemy, a conventional campaign would, quite counterproductively, bolster the legitimacy and credibility of the enemy in the eyes of the population from which it now draws its support. We can only eradicate the enemy through a *creative, unconventional guerrilla* warfare campaign of *absolutely fucking relentless attrition.*

A conventional military campaign would mean the

application of air power. We have seen how this works. We "liberate" cities by leveling them. Just look at Kobani. A conventional military campaign would mean a large, occupying army trying to take and hold cities and towns and infrastructure and territory from an unconventional enemy. That will go nowhere fast unless an obscenely large number of troops is employed. Didn't we learn something in our not-so-distant history about trying to take and hold territory from an unconventional enemy? It would also mean kicking in doors and clearing houses. This is one of the very tactics that rallies the enemy and inspires new recruits. It is also of dubious utility in a situation where the enemy blends with and moves freely among the noncombatant population and often has the support of said noncombatant population.

The answer is a *guerrilla* ground war fought by small units not occupying large swaths of Arab/Muslim lands, not kicking in doors and killing or disrupting the lives of noncombatants, and not destroying infrastructure and leveling cities, *but relentlessly attritting the enemy*. You don't have to take and hold any damn thing - not a province nor a city nor a patch of ground. You simply kill the enemy where they are until they simply aren't anymore. Small units have extreme advantages over a large army in the prosecution of a guerrilla war. Remember that Team Swandog advance teams roamed the Islamic State theater of operation for six months undetected. Small units can move about freely and undetected whereas large numbers of conventional troops could never hope to. That's just the beginning.

There are many tactical advantages to small unit action as opposed to the conventional application of force with this particular enemy, and understanding the enemy and the drivers of the enemy's actions allows us to capitalize on the many advantages of small unit action as well as to turn what the enemy perceives to be its strengths into fatal weaknesses. The inertia of large, conventional units, together with the tactics they must use, would make any campaign to defeat the Islamic State and eradicate militant Islam a *generational* war – a decades-long war. A small guerrilla force would not be burdened by such inertia. A concerted and highly organized campaign by a force of 3,000 warriors with elite training in guerrilla warfare, operating in small units, and acting pursuant to the correct strategy could eliminate the Islamic State in 9-24 months depending on the level of funding and eradicate militant Islam – including toppling the current regime in Iran – in well under a decade. I will say it right now; Team Swandog could destroy the Islamic State, topple the Iranian Regime, and eradicate the entire ideology of militant Islam in five to six years and do it for under $60B.

A light guerrilla force, dispossessed of the inertia of a large force and the cumbersome rules of engagement that hobble modern state action, would be the most effective means by which to eliminate this enemy. Team Swandog has already proven that small units can move about at will, with total freedom and with little threat of detection, in the IS theater of operation. Rather than concentrating large numbers of forces to engage the enemy in pitched battles, we can disburse small units all across the theater of operation to engage the enemy *every day and everywhere – even deep within its territory* - with coordinated harassing attacks, sniping, sabotage, supply chain disruption, resource denial, and so forth. We could easily rack up hundreds of enemy KIA every day and do so in a way that lets them know we can indeed hit them anywhere and everywhere we choose. This type of conflict is referred to as low-intensity, but it doesn't seem very low-intensity to those on the receiving end.

We are the wasp that has evolved to formulate its venom to be deadly to its prey. We have developed tactics that are impossible for the Islamic State to defend against, and we continue to do so. Our repertoire of available tactics is mind boggling even to me. There would be no learning curve for IS. They will never know what to expect. We can change our game every day for a year, and we can adapt to any way they could possibly change their behavior in response to our operations. The Islamic State trying to defend against our operations will be as futile as trying to swat down a swarm of attacking yellowjackets. Yellowjackets are small and almost impossible to see until they are already on you. They are fast, unpredictable, and extremely aggressive, and they will tear you the fuck up. The giant, lumbering elephant that is state action executed by large forces may indeed be quite destructive, but it is indiscriminately so and it will no more likely stomp out the Islamic State than elephants will stomp out every meerkat in Africa. It is much better to unleash a relentless swarm of pissed off yellowjackets.

One of the greatest advantages of this approach is the deleterious effect it will *in very short order* have on the enemy. Not only does it attrit the enemy, thereby reducing their overall number, but it has other effects that are just as crippling. It erodes the morale of the enemy, making them less effective. Morale cannot long hold up when you are being attacked day in and day out, all across and deep within your territory, by an enemy you never see until it's too late, and there's nothing you can do to stop it. Morale will quickly be swirling the toilet bowl, and, just as important, recruiting will suffer. The romance of the cause and its rapid success have been extremely effective recruiting tools, but there's nothing romantic or successful about being continually attritted by an enemy acting with apparent total freedom of movement and near impunity in your homeland.

Eroding morale and frustrating recruiting are just the start. What happens when the Arab-Islamic world – not to mention the rest of the world – sees the Islamic State being beaten day in and day out in such a manner by a far inferior number of *infidels*? You guessed it. The idea of IS being Allah's soldiers in Allah's cause will come into question.

How could they be Allah's soldiers in Allah's cause if Allah is allowing them to have their ass handed to them by a small number of infidel Americans? If they are Allah's soldiers in Allah's cause, then the god of those making war against them must be more powerful than Allah. Think about that for a minute.

The more we attrit them in this way, the more we delegitimize and discredit the movement and its ideology. The fighters we don't kill will be so discredited that no one will support them and so disillusioned with a cause no longer seen as legitimate that they will desert. The ideology of jihad will first be marginalized in the Arab-Islamic world and then completely delegitimized as group after group is defeated by a few infidels. The ideology of jihad and the subjugation of the world to Islam and Sharia law will die within Islam. What will be left is a truly peaceful and tolerant Islam. Whether that reflects the Qu'ran and the Hadith is irrelevant. The ideology cannot be allowed to survive.

I know some of you are still wondering what makes me so confident in the tactics that Team Swandog has developed and continues to develop. I get my confidence from the fact that we know the enemy. You cannot capitalize on the nature and characteristics of your enemy if you refuse to know them. I would venture to say that there are few if any who know the enemy and grasp its nature and characteristics better than Team Swandog.

Capitalizing on the Nature and Characteristics of the Enemy

The first step is to admit that the enemy is militant Islam. We simply must understand this about our enemy. I have said before and will say again that we can turn what the enemy perceives as its strengths against it and make them weaknesses for us to exploit fully and completely. The debate as to whether it is true Islam or a perversion is irrelevant to the task of using the enemy's ideology against it. Denying the Islamic nature and drivers of the jihad is nothing less than the pinnacle of stupidity. I'm going to say it again ... institutionalized idiocy. We cannot exploit our enemy's inherent vulnerabilities unless we know our enemy, and knowing that our enemy is Islamic and is driven by Islamic ideology (whether perverted or not) is absolutely crucial. It gives us an advantage that cannot be dealt with, because to address this advantage would require a fundamental change in the core faith and motivation of the enemy. That is simply not a possibility. Because of the enemy's Islamic nature, there are true constants in its character which we can exploit to destroy them. Knowing the enemy is Islamic, we can formulate the strategy and tactics needed to best engage them in this guerrilla war, to erode their morale, to frustrate their recruiting, and to ultimately delegitimize and discredit them for all time.

I am not going to get into specific tactical advantages the Islamic nature of the enemy hands us on a silver platter, but there are many. The educated strategist and enlightened tactician will make the unapologetic and uninhibited exploitation of such weaknesses inherent in the very core of his enemy the number one factor in planing his enemy's demise. The more you understand your enemy, the more you understand how to end him. I understand this enemy very well, and my team and I will soon set about the business of ending them.

Capitalizing on the Nature of the Jihad

I use the word jihad for a reason. This *is* a holy war. This *is* a religious war. There is no way around it. It is militant Islam against Christianity, Judaism, and every other "infidel" faith on the planet. When your enemy wants to kill you *because of your religion*, and they are motivated *by their religion* to kill or subjugate everyone who will not *convert to their religion*, you are in a religious war, like it or not. We cannot just decide this isn't a religious war simply because we find the notion of being in a religious war distasteful to our idiotic sense of geopolitical and geosocial correctness. The fact that the concept of religious war does not fit with some cockeyed world view doesn't mean that the defending party to a religious war should refuse to recognize and accept the religious nature of the war. Far from it.

What advantage is there in blindly (and quite stupidly) refusing to acknowledge the religious nature of the war? Absolutely none. It is an impediment to victory. That doesn't mean there is not *perceived* advantage. That perceived advantage, though, is not a strategic one or even a tactical one. It is a geopolitical and geosocial one, and it is only perceived and not real. Denying the religious nature of this war allows us to demonstrate to the world a pretense of tolerance and enlightenment. We're not the bad guys. We love Islam and would never be at war with Islam, because it is a peaceful and tolerant religion. We are so above such a thing that we deny the overtly Islamic (although extreme fundamentalist) nature of our enemy and our enemy's motivations. Hey, look at us! Look at how bigoted we are *not*! We are so *not* bigoted and so civilized and enlightened that we are simply beyond the idea of religious war altogether. The world has become so nuts – so completely insane – that our primary concern is not defending ourselves from an enemy bent by religious ideology on the eradication of our way of life but instead behaving toward the world and even *toward that enemy* in such a way that nobody will see us as bigots. What the fuck?! Am I the only one who thinks it's more than a little off that we are the only party to this jihad who denies it's religious nature? The enemy – the offending party – is very clear and open about the religious nature of the war and about its religious motivations.

So, what advantage is there, then, in acknowledging and accepting the religious nature of this war – this jihad? Plenty. Acceptance of the religious nature of this war allows us to tap into a tremendous source of support – the churches and the religious. We can rally support not just around the flag but around the defense of freedom of religion from a religious faction that would see all other religions and their practitioners ended. The more popular support for your fight, the better. The more ardent the support, the better. There is tremendous advantage in casting a war as one waged by one religion or religious faction against another. In this case, we don't have to cast it that way. Our enemy aggressor has done that for us, and quite emphatically so. Fighting for country is one thing. Fighting for *God and country* is entirely another.

In the context of Team Swandog's solution – private sector as it is – there is even more advantage in accepting the religious nature of this war. There is no funding from the government. In fact, this administration will probably do everything it can to stop us. We need the support of the churches. The funding for this private sector solution comes primarily from businesses whose leaders love America and understand the threat posed by this enemy. The churches, though, are a tremendous source of funding. Churches and religious people who understand the religious nature of this war and the threat this enemy poses to their free exercise of their religion are phenomenal support. We already have a good number of churches taking special collections to help us win this war. We need the rest, and stopping this insane denial of the religious nature of the war is key to winning it.

The reality is that we *are* in a religious war against an

enemy whose goal is to end our religion and subjugate the whole world to their brand of Islam and Sharia law. The nature of a war as a religious or secular war is not dependent upon the agreement of the warring parties. To think so is naivete in the extreme. The aggressor sets the nature. If we don't accept that, we have no hope of victory, because we are just too far gone into the abyss of idiocy that is political and social correctness. We are not doomed, though, if we will shake off the stupor of denial, stop making supremely important the price of our stock on the world market of political and social opinion, and evaluate strategies without our blinders of political and social correctness affixed firmly over our eyes.

ADDRESSING ONLINE RADICALIZATION

Especially after the deaths of four Marines and a Sailor in Chattanooga at the hands of a recently radicalized Islamic militant, there has been a lot of media and pundit attention given to the issue of online radicalization. Most it seems want to further empower the government to spy on our online communications. There have been some very good suggestions for the use of HUMINT, and they are to be applauded. Nothing, though, will have nearly as deleterious an effect on online radicalization that Team Swandog's strategy. Nothing will reduce online radicalization more than the discrediting and delegitimizing of the militant groups and their underlying ideologies. They are masters of messaging. We have to be better not only with our message but our messaging strategy.

Every one of my men will be equipped with a body camera, and there will be others documenting every aspect of our fight against IS as well. Every kill and every success will be posted online for the world to see. With each passing day, we will provide to the world more evidence that we are indeed kicking ass. Being a part of IS or any other militant Islamic group will be less and less attractive. Like I have said, people want to join winning causes, not losing ones. People want to join glorious and romantic causes, and there's nothing glorious or romantic about getting the shit kicked out of you day in and day out with the evidence splashed across the World Wide Web. We will spread to the entire world the proof that Allah cannot be on the side of these evil-minded but pathetic and cowardly douchebags. If he was, he would surely not let a band of infidels much smaller in number than they kick their butts all over their own land and put it on the Internet.

It may seem harsh and gruesome and maybe even inhuman to post pictures and videos of our successes online, but doing so is the best way to win the messaging war and discredit and delegitimize the enemy. Discrediting and delegitimizing the enemy is the best way to stop online radicalization and recruiting. It sure beats the hell out of giving the FBI and the NSA more power to spy on us. Why is it that, in the face of danger, our first reaction is always to see what freedoms we can sacrifice in order to purchase the *idea* of safety and security?

IN SUMMATION

The campaign to eradicate militant Islam must begin with its flagship organization, the Islamic State. It's a statement victory. If we can eliminate the biggest and baddest of the hoard of militant Islamic organizations, none of the others stand a chance. Taking out IS first is going to have a massive effect on the will and efficacy of the remainder of the militant Islamic organizations, be they Shia or Sunni. This will only increase as we take out one group after the other, progressing through the roster of Militant Islam as we see fit. As we move to the organizations directly supported by Iran, we will likely encounter Iranian Quds forces, but they are no match for the training and tactics of Team Swandog. As the war must begin with the Islamic State, it must end with Iran. After having vanquished group after group and significantly discredited and delegitimized jihadism and its supporting ideologies, we can work with the resistance in Iran to quickly and relatively easily topple the regime. By the end of the war, we would have greatly eroded support for what is already a weak regime in terms of the support of its people. This regime has been perilously close to an end before without help from the West. (A testament to the weakening of the regime is its invigorated quest for a nuclear weapon.) A further weakened regime could not long stand in the face of a strengthened resistance aided and trained by us.

So, that's how it's done. That's how you destroy the Islamic State, eradicate militant Islam for good, and end an evil regime in Iran while relegating Hamas and Hezbollah to the pages of history. All of the underpinnings of this strategy are sound – rock solid indeed. No other strategy comes close to the likelihood of succeeding that this strategy has. Every other strategy advanced suffers from one or more of the fatal ailments of denial, institutionalized idiocy, conventional thought, fiscal impossibility, or just plain fantasy. It's past time to start thinking outside the box and get to the business of winning the war before it's too late and we are in fact inescapably doomed.

7
Jihad!
Call to Action

It is high time we stop relying on the idiots in Washington to do something about this clear and present danger - this existential threat to our existence – that is the Islamic State and militant Islam. In a year of combating IS, all the brain trust of our government and our generals have been able to come up with is a half-baked strategy that is really only more of the same. It's just more of the misguided idiocy that has grown militant Islam twenty-fold in the last 13 years and has spawned the Islamic State, Boko Haram, and many other militant Islamic organizations. **We can no longer rely on the governments of the Unites States and the modern West to solve the problem**. They have demonstrated themselves quite incapable, and the threat continues to grow in numbers and power and advance on our homeland. We have to take matters into our own hands and implement the private sector solution. We the People have to raise the men and the money and go do the job which must be done if we are to remain a free people much longer.

WHY TEAM SWANDOG INSTEAD OF MILITARY SPECIAL OPERATIONS?

Okay. I know a lot of you are thinking that the governments of the U.S. and the modern West could be convinced to magically emerge from their stupor of institutionalized idiocy and we could accomplish this strategy using the Navy SEALS, Army Green Berets, Marine Force Recon, Army Rangers, MARSOC, DEVGRU, and CAG/Delta. Not so fast. This idea has some fatal flaws. First, it would still be state action and would have the same impediments to success I have discussed herein – pandering to perceived world opinion, fuzzy objective, stupid political rules of engagement, and perception in the Arab-Islamic world, just to recall a few. Second, these may indeed be special operations units, but they are still way, way to conventional to properly execute such a strategy. Anyone who has worked with these units knows that even the Tier 1 units are not unconventional warfare units in the sense of this strategy of true guerrilla fighting. True guerrilla fighting is the only cure for the cancer of militant Islam. I am not sure this is even something that can be grasped by the command structure. The operators, yes, but the command structure … I highly doubt it. Too much politics. Too much institutionalized idiocy. I also have reason to doubt the intelligence of the tacticians and operational planners responsible for these "special" operations. They seem to be addicted to the war machine. What I mean by that is I don't believe they could walk away from the trappings of a big state military or even have the ability to think outside of that context.

How many times have we seen these units ingress/infiltrate and egress/exfiltrate via Black Hawk helicopter? When that's what you have, that's what you go to, but it is often the *least intelligent means* of infiltrating and exfiltrating denied-access territory this side of a damn ticker tape parade advertised in every paper for weeks ahead of time. Maybe it takes a background in clandestine operations to see that. Maybe it takes a different way of thinking and of looking at things. You can have all the advanced technology and latest toys, and your thinking can still be stale. Unless an operation is extremely – and I mean *extremely* - time-critical, there is a handful of better ways to get in and out.

This is just one example of many drawbacks of conventional SpecOps thinking that I have observed and that special operators have privately complained to me about for years. I believe it only shows that the mindset in our military – even special operations - is nowhere near the mindset that is absolutely essential to carry out this strategy. Though I am certain our troops could adapt, I do not believe the *institution* of the military has that ability in the slightest. As mentioned earlier in this book, it is not the unconventional, creative, forward-thinkers who advance into the command structure in the military. It is not the innovators or the restless-minded. It is the conformists. It is the politically savvy. If you don't see this, then you don't have much knowledge of and experience with the military. It is conformity that is rewarded, and when conformity is rewarded, there is no incentive for innovative thought.

ACTION, NOT WORDS

The time for tough talking is long past, and it is time to act ... past time in fact. Tough talking gets us nowhere. It's the same with endless debate. We have been debating strategies on cable news for a year now while the Islamic State has increased it's territory, recruiting, and revenue streams. Of course, the strategy we are debating is just an IS strategy. Nobody ventures to offer a strategy for the eradication of militant Islam as a whole – except for Team Swandog. We can continue to discuss and debate the merits of the various strategies advanced by the talking heads, most if not all of which rely on the government, military, and modern Western world to get their collective heads out of their asses. That is an option. We can keep pumping words out of our mouths and keep pounding the keys on our laptops, because God knows that's what draws viewers and readers ... or we can take the first best option and put it into operation. This is a strategy which doesn't need a single damn politician. All it needs is patriotic, free-thinking people who can take the blinders off long enough to see reality.

I am calling for volunteers with military experience. Special operations experience is a plus but not essential. My men and I can train just about anyone with a military background to be an effective practitioner of the kind of warfare in which we will be engaged. Patriotism and an open mind are a must. Some concepts will have to be trained out of you. If you are a veteran, I am calling on you. I know you have already done your part, and I know it isn't fair of anyone to expect you to do more, but your country needs you to do more.

I am calling on volunteers to work in noncombat roles. We have the need for people to work in areas from logistics to public relations to fundraising. Fundraising is absolutely critical. We don't have our hands in the bottomless pockets of any government. We need people to help us raise the money we need to eradicate this enemy before it eradicates us.

I am calling on doctors and nurses and surgeons to work in our field medical units and keep our guys healthy and patch them up when needed. The pay is okay, and you can set the length of your rotation in theater. We need you.

I am calling on every church in the country to realize that we are engaged in a religious war and *must do what is necessary* to ensure not only our own right to practice and indeed to live but that of our posterity as well. There comes a time when you have to fight not just for your life or for your country but for God as well. That time is now. Militant Islam is making war on Christianity, Judaism, and America, along with the rest of the modern West. I am calling on every church in America to support our fight against this enemy *which desires nothing more than the extinction of every religion but their brand of Islam.* I urge you to start taking special collections for the war against the Islamic State and militant Islam this Sunday and every Sunday thereafter. Team Swandog will let you know how to get it to us.

I am calling on big businesses all across the nation to support us in this war. The Islamic State can be defeated for less than the government has already wasted training the Iraqi Army. I am calling on small businesses, too, but even just a handful of the Fortune 500 companies could fully fund this war against evil and not even miss the money, but small businesses are important to this effort as well. I know in my heart there are enough patriotic and wise CEOs and CFOs out there to win this war by making sure my men and I have the things we need to fight it. I know they are out there, because some have already supported Team Swandog advance teams working in the IS theater. Some have already believed in the cause and the necessity of this type of action. We need many more. We need you.

Despite the strategy and the tactics and despite the dedication and patriotism of the men and women of Team

Swandog, we cannot win this war without money. It's just a sad truth. If you get that this is not a war our government can win, and if you understand that we must defeat them on their ground before they come defeat us on ours, then sign up to do your part today, whatever that part may be. There is no contribution that is insignificant. Every dollar sent and every hour volunteered, and every skill that can be provided will help to win this jihad. We must act without delay. Visit our website to find out how.

NGOTeamSwandog.org

I would love to see the involvement of the governments of some of the Arab and African countries that are dealing with the Islamic State and Boko Haram as well as Al Qaeda and Al-Shabaab get involved as well. Every peaceful Arab country benefits from a stable Arab region. The same holds true for Africa. Every peaceful African country benefits from the extermination of Boko Haram and the Islamic State as well as AQIM. Every one of these countries could and indeed should have a major role in the funding of this strategy.

There are several advantages to working with Team Swandog to carry out this strategy. There is not only the obvious advantage of achieving greater stability and ridding the world of this menace, but here are more subtle benefits as well. Partnering with Team Swandog is much more affordable than going it alone with conventional direct action. It also allows the governments to distance themselves from the action publicly while funding it privately. They can stay above the fray, so to speak. It is politically expedient.

It could all be indirect as well. A government could enter into a contract with Team Swandog for the training of some of its forces in this specialized type of guerrilla warfare. Those forces may be trained in the IS theater of operations, Yemen, Nigeria, or wherever militant Islam threatens fee people and their governments. Everybody wins. Well, not everybody. The Islamic State and Boko Haram and Hamas and Hezbollah and Iran lose. All of militant Islam looses, but Africa wins. The Arab world wins. The entire free world wins. Liberty wins, and so does Islam as a peaceful and tolerant religion.

Team Swandog welcomes the involvement of the government of any and every interested country. Together we can destroy IS and Boko Haram. Together we can end Al Qaeda and Al-Shabaab. Together we can triumph over evil and make the world a safe place for people of all religions. Have your representative sit down with me for one day. You will not be disappointed.

8
Critics, Detractors, Liars, Haters & Just Plain Assholes

Has anybody noticed that we live in a very negative, distrusting, even paranoid and just plain mean-spirited world? That which doesn't fit the mold is subject to the most outrageous, uninformed, and unethical attacks, often under the guise of protecting the people. Many who disagree with what I have to say and with my efforts to defeat the Islamic State and eradicate militant Islam have been attacking me and will continue to do so. This is to be expected, since I do not discuss my background or how I came about my expertise in this field. If someone attempts something extraordinary, they damn sure better have the right pedigree and resume, or they will be the subject of vicious attacks, and the attackers will urge that you immediately discount *with extreme prejudice* whatever the person has to say without even looking to see if what they say has any validity at all. Of course. That's just common sense. We all know that nobody who doesn't point to X, Y, Z and a dozen other proofs of their *bona fides* could possibly have anything worthwhile to say, right? Wrong!

Our world is one where the elite tell us that nobody is extraordinary on their own. They can only possibly become that way under the tutelage of people more extraordinary than they, and if they cannot supply proof of such tutelage, they are frauds. There are also no good reasons anyone may choose not to disclose the circumstances of such tutelage. The proof is no longer in the pudding; it's in the pedigree. Arguments are no longer critically analyzed. What's the point? Why waste your time critically analyzing the arguments of someone who either does not have or chooses not to disclose and discuss the verifiable *bona fides* the elite find requisite to having an opinion worth a shit?

That position is total bullshit. If it was valid, then we would still be cave men, because, if we are only qualified to the extent we are taught by others more qualified than ourselves, there would be no advancements – *ever*. There couldn't be. Instead of evolving and advancing, culture would devolve and disintegrate. People are not perfect learners or perfect teachers, so with each successive generation, there would be a *decrease* rather than an *increase* in knowledge and qualification to do or think anything. Our world and our species have only advanced because we are *decidedly not* bound by the knowledge and qualifications of our teachers.

There *are* naturals, and there *are* also people who are supremely qualified but have legitimate reasons for not disclosing or discussing how they became so qualified. If you are either one of these or both, and you try to do something extraordinary or advance a novel perspective – regardless of the validity of your argument and perhaps even *because* of it – the elite and those who perceive themselves to be elite will hunt you down and shoot you like a rabid dog. There will, from critics, detractors, liars, haters, and just plain assholes, be a relentless onslaught of fallacious reasoning which will be taken by most as Gospel.

THE CRITICS

There will be critics, and that would be fine if that were the extent of it and if a person could have their knowledge and expertise judged *by their work product instead of by their pedigree*. A person's argument or position or conclusion should be judged **on its own merits and validity and nothing else**. Instead, unless you are someone the elite are prepared to recognize as an expert, it will be judged on everything but its own merit. The critics are the more fair-minded of the bunch, and they will at least make a strong pretense of looking at the merits of what you have to say. However, even the critics will, once they see your argument offends their sociopolitical preconceptions, lob their own attacks of logical fallacies.

The main fallacy of logic employed by the critics will also be employed by the detractors, the liars, the haters, and the just plain assholes, but with more vigor and abandon. This logical fallacy is the bedrock upon which the entire world view of the elite, and unfortunately a large portion of our culture, is based ... a type of genetic fallacy known as the appeal to accomplishment. The genetic fallacy involves accepting or rejecting a conclusion not based on the validity of the argument but based instead on the source. If you have accomplishments you can crow about, you are obviously right, and your argument is valid. Your conclusion should be adopted. If you do not have accomplishments you can crow about, you are obviously wrong, and your argument cannot possibly be valid. Your conclusion should be rejected out of hand based on your *perceived* lack of accomplishments.

THE DETRACTORS

The detractors are worse. They don't even pretend to evaluate what you have to say on its merits. They assume from the very beginning your argument or position has none, so why bother? They instead focus their energy trying to defeat your argument not by merit by fallacy of logic after fallacy of logic. The detractors employ the genetic fallacy right off the bat. Your conclusion is rejected solely because of you – or rather false preconceptions of you held by those encountering your argument who don't even know a thing about you - rather than any actual lack of merit in your argument. Your premises could be perfect and your argument completely valid, but that wouldn't matter, because what you have to say will never meet with critical analysis simply because of its source - you.

The faulty assumption that will be trotted out by the detractors and which will be made the centerpiece of their attack on you is born of an appeal to silence, which is another fallacy of logic. Say you claim to be accomplished in a certain field, to be a natural in that field, or both, but for perfectly legitimate reasons, you decline to disclose or discuss the basis of your expertise. The appeal to silence says since you do not offer proof of your expertise, you are obviously not an expert and should not be trusted. This, of course, is not valid reasoning. As stated, there could well be valid reasons an expert may decline to prove his expertise by evidence other than the merits of his argument. The detractors don't want the argument evaluated on its merits, though, because they have their agenda. If the appeal to accomplishment and the appeal to silence don't work, they will resort to additional fallacies employed by the liars, the haters, and the just plain assholes. Let's take them one by one.

THE LIARS

Next there are the liars. The liars will employ the appeal to accomplishment and the appeal to silence, but the main weapon in their arsenal of fallacies of logic is the *ad hominem*. They will attack you rather than your argument, thinking that demonizing you makes your argument invalid and your conclusion false. Not only will they uncover every mistake in your past, but they will tell whatever lies they believe will sufficiently undermine your legitimacy. Then they will shift the burden to you to prove their assertions false when it is really on them to prove their claims true. Sadly, many people fall for this shit. The *ad hominem* is a fallacy because good people have bad ideas, and bad people have good ideas. Whether someone is perceived as a good or bad person is irrelevant to the merits of their position. When the *ad hominem* is based on lies conjured up for the purpose of discrediting you, the fallacy is even more egregious.

Unfortunately, in the court of public opinion, a person is not innocent until proven guilty *but is instead guilty until proven innocent*. This ugly truth about our culture is what gives the liars such an advantage.

THE HATERS

The haters are even worse. The critics and the detractors and the liars may have at least partially sincere philosophical objections to your argument and conclusion arising out of their strong desire for political and social correctness. They may be justified, in their world view, in attacking you and your position. The haters just hate you and everything you stand for. They will use all the fallacies the prior groups use plus one more. They won't stop with lying about you and basing their *ad hominem* attacks on their lies. They will also use the appeal to the stone, which a lot of people fall for. The appeal to the stone asserts that something is absurd without offering any evidence that it is so. They will label your position as absurd, and when asked to show why it is absurd, they will merely state that it is quite obviously absurd to anyone with a brain. Because they hate you and everything you stand for, they won't come within a mile of your argument to test it. It is just dismissed as absurd because it does not fit the world view they seek to advance. We see this a lot in the climate change debate where those who advance the idea of anthropogenic global warming label as absurd any argument against their conclusion that global warming is not only real but man-made as well. They don't attack the opposing argument's validity; they just label it as absurd and use it's supposed obvious absurdity as proof that it is absurd. Anyone up for some circular reasoning? You will see this a lot in the national discussion of the Islamic State and militant Islam. Those who believe overwhelming force is the only way to go will dismiss the Team Swandog strategy as absurd simply because, to them, anything less than overwhelming force is absurd. The social conscience crowd will dismiss any application of military or paramilitary force as absurd because they believe any use of such force to be absurd. Others will dismiss this private sector solution as absurd in their belief that anything other than government-military action is automatically absurd. In every case, it will be an appeal to the stone.

THE JUST PLAIN ASSHOLES

Last we have the just plain assholes. They will use every fallacy of logic in the book. These are the elite – the self-anointed intelligentsia. They don't necessarily hate you. They just don't believe anyone other than them ever had a good idea, and they feel threatened when someone who hasn't passed their expert test asserts an actual novel idea. If it didn't come from their brain, it has to be shit, and they will try their hardest to convince the world it is so. They won't stop with the appeal to accomplishment or the appeal to silence or the *ad hominem* or the appeal to the stone. They employ other fallacies of logic as well, such as the red herring and the straw man. They will morph from the *ad hominem* into the red herring. They will make the discussion about you – actually about the false preconceptions and assumptions and lies about you - and most certainly not about the merits of your argument. No matter what you say, they will always have an answer that may seem legit but is as fallacious as all their other crap. They will declare you a phony or a fraud or a liar or a poser or a flat-out loon based on little or nothing (usually nothing) and use that false conclusion to prove that your argument is crap. Many will buy it, unfortunately.

MY RESPONSE

This is the only response you will ever get from me to the attacks that have been coming from the start and will keep coming and even intensify. I cannot waste all of my time refuting fallacious attacks on me and my strategy. That would be a full-time job and then some. It would be worse than whack-a-mole, and I refuse to get caught up in such a fool's errand and play the game of those who are themselves tilting at windmills.

Ever since the first publicity for Team Swandog, I have been the subject of every kind of attack you could imagine. Every one has used fallacies of logic. Most have also used lies and assumptions based on incomplete evidence, and I have not responded. As I have said, there is simply no way I can get trapped into refuting every attack as they come. There have been many, and there will be many, many more. The point of this chapter is to demonstrate that they are all completely invalid and that what I have to say in this book should be evaluated on its merits rather than some unjustified and baseless preconception of me.

I am indeed an expert in intelligence, special operations, and unconventional warfare. My specialties include sniper, close combat, and psychological warfare as well as guerrilla warfare and the improvisational development of small unit tactics. I am also a natural when it comes to guerrilla warfare and the development of unconventional strategy and tactics. I have the education and training to accomplish everything I say I can and more. I was trained primarily by Paramilitary Operations Officers from the CIA's National Clandestine Service but also by Marines, Green Berets, and operators from the Navy SEALs, MARSOC, and CAG/Delta as well. There are many reasons I decline to discuss how I came about this level of expertise. I don't have to discuss them with anyone. **The proof of my expertise is in my work product – in the strategy and tactics I have developed along with others on my team.** Any expert in this field who reads this book with an open mind and sits down with me for half a day to discuss the strategy and tactics I advocate – without prejudice - will be convinced. The proof *is* in the pudding.

I don't disclose where my training and expertise come from for a couple of reasons. First, there's really very, very little I can tell you, and there's none of it you can verify no matter who you are or what connections you have. Anything I could tell you would tend to make the discussion more about me and about the structure and function of our nation's intelligence community and the people in it. That leads into the second reason. The discussion should be about the strategy I put forward and not about me or anything I may or may not have been involved in. As it turns out, many want to make the discussion about me instead of my work product, anyway. I'm damned if I do and damned if I don't. I chose don't, and I'm sticking to it.

Again, the proof of my expertise is **in my work product** – the strategy and tactics that will destroy the Islamic State and eradicate militant Islam. Evaluate my work on its own merits. That's all I ask. Unfortunately, we live in a culture of negativity and distrust and suspicion where arguments are not evaluated on their merits as much as they are on the perceived qualities of the ones advancing them. If your argument supports a cause that needs to raise money, the suspicion and presupposition of criminal motives can be *absolutely destructive* to you and your reputation and your cause.

I have been labeled a fraud and a con artist and a phony and a loon – all by people who have very limited knowledge of and experience with me, **if any at all**. This negative and distrustful culture we live in leads many who are unfamiliar with me or don't have full knowledge of me and who and what I am to make assumptions they have no business making and to act on those assumptions. Many people live their entire lives by the genetic fallacy and assume the fact that I have never served in the *military*

proper means I am utterly unqualified to speak to this issue
let alone develop a strategy and tactics to destroy IS and
eradicate militant Islam. So, naturally I must be a fraud,
right?

Others just lie and/or completely mischaracterize me.
A lot of these people are self-appointed watchdogs who
presume to take it upon themselves to "protect" the public
from ideas they deem in their woefully lacking intelligence
and education to be invalid or people they deem in their
pathetically uninformed minds to be unstable or posers or
con artists. With reckless abandon and even hubristic glee
they let slip their dogs of war upon anyone who offends their
infantile sensibilities. It is worse when yours is a cause you
need to raise money for. Oh, God, it is worse! Everyone
trying to raise money for some extraordinary cause is seen as
a Ponzi or a Madoff wannabe. If you'd like to see this in
action, just go out and try to raise funds for a new cause. See
how many people come out of the woodwork to tear you
down. It will be faster if you don't flaunt a fancy pedigree
and full resume or if you haven't lead a spotless life.

I am no Ponzi or Madoff. I am no Satan. Nor am I by
any stretch of the imagination a saint or a choir boy. The
work ahead of us in this jihad – the work which must be
done to preserve liberty against the tyranny of militant Islam
– is no work for saints or choir boys. I have a past. Am I
proud of everything I have done in my life? No. Are you
proud of everything you have done? Hell, I have done a lot

of things I shouldn't have done and so have each of you. So has everyone who is trying to tear me down. I have hurt people. Sometimes it was intentional, but most often it was unintentional. If we're telling the truth here, the same can be said for each and every person reading this book. We all have wrongs we have not made right. In my case, everyone I have wronged and many I have not wronged but who feel I have wronged them will come out to tear me down. They will bring their claims and their evidence, but keep one thing in mind. I do not have a criminal record. I have never even been charged with any scam or con or fraud, let alone convicted of such a thing. I in fact hold a license to carry a concealed handgun, for which I had to pass FBI and State Police background checks. Still, my accusers will come. Some will claim to have had past dealings with me, and some will be telling the truth. Some will claim to have intimate knowledge of or even a familial relationship with me. They all have their own ax to grind, and none of them truly know me.

Consider something for a moment. Don't you think a person who is in a position to have the expertise my work product proves I have would be the last person in the world anyone would expect to have such expertise? Wouldn't it be wise for that person to live his life in such a manner as to be the one person everyone around him or who has dealt with him would be certain to their bones has no such qualifications? Do you think a person with the expertise my

work product proves I have would find advantage and
security in appearing to all outward observers as the last
person to suspect of possessing such expertise? Do you think
the past of such a person would be pristine or checkered?
Would everything in that person's life and past be
misdirection? Would the trail lead in a dozen different
directions? Would there be a reason for him to keep even
those closest to him in the dark about this part of him?

Suppose for a moment that you are a foreign agent
here looking for someone who has the expertise I have –
maybe a certain someone. Suppose further that the
information you had on this certain someone was sketchy,
but you had an idea where to look. In your looking, would
you suspect the one who by all outward appearances has
never held down a job for more than a year. Would you
suspect the ne'er-do-well and college drop-out? Would you
suspect the shady dealer who has made enemies? Would you
suspect the mental patient? Would you suspect the local
Walter Mitty? Could there be an advantage for someone who
gained the expertise I have in the usual way to appear to
some to be one of these people and appear to others to be
another? Could there be method to the apparent madness?
Could it all just be a smoke screen?

The fact is **there is no claim which may be made
against me in an attempt to discredit me that is
based on complete knowledge.** Not a one. Further,
even if they were all true – every last one – it would be

irrelevant to the critical analysis of the strategy and tactics I advance to win the jihad in which we are now engaged. If my strategy is to be discredited based on fallacies of logic such as the genetic fallacy, the appeal to accomplishment, the appeal to silence, the appeal to the stone, the ad hominem, and the red herring, then we must also fully and completely discredit the work of people like Copernicus, Galileo, Albert Einstein and John Nash, the presidencies of John F. Kennedy and Bill Clinton just for starters, not to mention the lives of John D. Rockefeller and Andrew Carnegie. If all arguments are to be evaluated by the perceived accomplishment, perceived moral scruples, and perceived perfect mental health of the person proffering them, then rare indeed is the argument that will be found valid.

My expertise is born out in my work product – the strategy and tactics I advance for the destruction of the Islamic State and the eradication of militant Islam. People will come out of the woodwork claiming all kinds of things. None of them – not even the ones who claim to be closest to me, are in a position to know the truth of me. Not even my own mother was aware of scars I bear from blades and bullets until just before the publication of this book when I showed them to her.

So, believe what you will from whatever source it comes, but if you think you have gotten the whole story from my attackers or from something you think you've uncovered or even from some tattoo I have, then you're a total fucking moron! Evaluate the strategy and the tactics I advance for the winning of this jihad being waged against us on their own merits. Let my work product speak for itself and stand by itself. Let the proof be in the pudding, then let the architect of the strategy set about the work of winning the jihad and eradicating the enemy once and for all.

Here's a special note to those people who believe they have discovered my full real name and physical address and have published them: **you are a special kind of evil**. You know I am engaged in an effort that makes me a target of particular interest to the Islamic State and every other militant Islamic organization, yet you take great pleasure in posting what you believe to be my name and physical address. You either *intend* to unnecessarily put me in mortal danger or actually get me killed, or you just don't care if your holier-than-thou *ad hominems* and genetic fallacy attacks do that, because it is far more important that you discredit me and thereby discredit my message. Again, you either fully intend to put me in grave danger or you don't mind doing it as long as you can discredit me. You are the lowest of the low.

You think if you can tell the world I live in a trailer park they will not give my strategy and claims of expertise any credibility, and it may turn out that you are successful. Does the truth that I actually live in a site-built home make my strategy any more valid? Not any more than living in a mobile home would make it invalid. Not any more than a job as a patent clerk made Einstein's science any less valid. Not any more than Madoff's success made him trustworthy. As far as I am concerned, you are indeed a special kind of evil, and the sooner you rot in Hell the better. It takes an especially low and evil kind of person to purposefully or recklessly do something you must believe will put a patriot in grave danger. The information is out there that there has already been one attempt on my life by Islamic militants which left me with a concussion and drugged and poisoned. This is the very reason I don't put my name and personal information out there publicly. By all means, help these people out by publishing what you believe to be my name and physical address. Go for it, and show the world what truly despicable pieces of shit you really are. Make your mother proud!

<u>ABOUT THE AUTHOR</u>

Swandog is an expert in intelligence, special operations, and unconventional/guerrilla warfare, with specialties in close combat, psychological warfare, sniper, small unit tactics, and improvisational tactics development. He is very highly educated in psychology, political science, economics, philosophy, and religion. He has a WAIS-IV (2010) full-scale IQ in the 93rd percentile with comprehension skills in the 99.7th percentile. In addition to elite intelligence, he has elite education and training in guerrilla warfare and improvised weaponry and tactics with uncanny perception and an astounding capacity for unconventional and creative thought.

Swandog considers himself both an Arkansan and a Vermonter. He currently lives in Arkansas, where he was a self-defense, close combat, and SERE instructor until he was elected by his peers to command what is now Team Swandog in 2014. He is a hunter and an advocate for individual liberties including gun rights. He is an Arkansas Razorbacks Football fan. Swandog is a devout Christian practicing New Covenant Theology.

Swandog speaks to groups large and small about militant Islam, the religious war they wage against us, and the strategy to win the war and eradicate the ideology from the planet. He is a plain-spoken, compelling, and often humorous speaker. If you are interested in booking Swandog to speak to your group, you can do so through the Team Swandog website at NGOTeamSwandog.org. Bear in mind that his fees are considerable, as he is in high demand. He also has considerable security requirements, because his leadership of Team Swandog and his forceful opposition to militant Islam make him a prime target.

SPECIAL THANKS

This book would not have been possible without the enduring support and inspiration so selflessly provided by the following:

Rick Blaine, Lt. John J. Dunbar, Col. Walter E. Kurtz, Buck Rogers, Earnest T. Bass, Dr. Peter Mann, Tristan Ludlow, Remington Steele, Morgan "Gator" Bodine, Andy Dufresne, Bob Wiley, Tyler Endicott, Lou Grant, Rowdy Burns, Bobby Boucher, Bo Brady, Calleigh Duquesne, Castor Troy, Prof. Charles Eppes, John Lee Pettimore, Harry Callahan, Kelly Garrett, Cullen Bohannon, Dr. Spencer Reid, Lydia Brenner, Martin Riggs, Jim Rockford, Gail Hartman, Harry Tasker, Col. Steve Austin, Claire Spencer, Tom Sawyer, Jack Reacher, Blake Carrington, Brian Earl Spilner, Benjamin Matlock, Cora Munro, B.A. Baracus, John Cutter, Thomas Magnum, Colleen McMurphy, Vincent Gambini, Arthur Fonzarelli, Gabe Walker, Sarah Connor, Norman Bates, Derek Zoolander, John Patrick Mason, Dan Tanna, Curtis Lowe, Nate Pope, Ilsa Lund, Clark Griswold, Prof. Lillian Diane Sloan, Jerry Maguire, Murphy Brown, Neal Caffrey, Lawson Russell, Ally McBeal, J.J. McClure, Virgil Tibbs, George Pratt, Rocky Balboa, Jack Torrance, Dave Skylark, Chase Gioberti, L.B. Jeffries, Ellen Ripley, Detective Frank Drebin, James Conway, Ziggy Stardust, Ryan Stone, Lee Stetson, Jessica Fletcher, Nash Bridges, Eric Draven, Captain

Jack Sparrow, Dagwood Bumstead, Michael Westen, Catherine Trammel, Richard O'Connell, Callie Cargill, Gregory Sumner, Dr. Daniel Jackson, Reno Raines, Madelyn Hayes, David Addison, Jr., Captain Louis Renault, Indrid Cold, Kevin Flynn, Memphis Raines, Alex Forrest, Sgt. Joe Friday, Jed Clampett, Avery Tolar, Michael Knight, Eric Matthews, Marty McFly, Dr. Gregory House, FBI Special Agent John Utah, Opie Taylor, Barnaby Jones, Doralee Rhodes, Jack Ryan, Benson Duboise, Anita Massengil, Ace Ventura, Edith Bunker, Dr. Sam Beckett, Daphne Moon, Indiana Jones, Jason Bourne, Lt. Theo Kojak, Daryll Lee Cullum, Dirk Pitt, Mike Hammer, Doctor Yuri Zhivago, Dana Scully, James Bond, Sgt. Clayton "Zeke" Anderson, Bobby McGee, Judge Milton C. Hardcastle, Willy Wonka, Philo Beddoe, Detective John Kimble, Blanche Devereaux, Dick Tracy, Harry Hogg, Casey Ryback, Lt. Hortio Caine, Nick Ryder, George Malley, Juno Skinner, Jack T. Colton, Rick Hunter, Dominic Toretto, Roy G. Biv, Detective Adrian Monk, Max Cady, Daisy Duke, Will Dormer, John Boy Walton, Forrest Gump, T.J. Hooker, Fred Krueger, Doogie Howser, Johnny B. Goode, Leslie Zevo, Patrick Jane, Constance Weldon Semple Carlyle, Jason McCabe, Monroe Ficus, Peyton Flanders, Dr. Hannibal Lecter, Sen. Jack S. Fogbound, Bryan Mills, Lt. Jordan O'Neill, Old Dan Tucker, Elka Ostrovsky, Leroy Brown, George Jefferson, J.R. Ewing, Rick Grimes, U.S. Marshal J.D. Cahill, Topper Harley, Sheriff Walt Longmire, Django Freeman, Steve McGarrett,

Arthur Bishop, B.J. McKay, Stroker Ace, Idgie Threadgoode, Keyser Söze, Henry Gondorff, Korben Dallas, Rick and A.J. Simon, Cordell Walker, Dr. Jordan Cavanaugh, Clark Kent, Ethylene Glycol, Luke Skywalker, Rufus Xavier Sarsaparilla, and John Jacob Jingleheimer Schmidt.

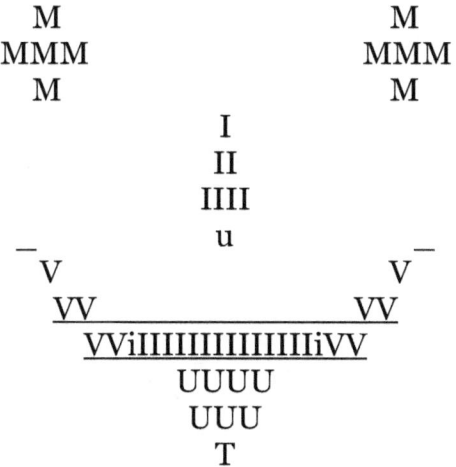

www.ingramcontent.com/pod-product-compliance
Lightning Source LLC
Chambersburg PA
CBHW070912290526
45795CB00001B/295